The Journal of Andrew Fuller Studies

Published in the United States of America by
by The Andrew Fuller Center for Baptist Studies
The Southern Baptist Theological Seminary
2825 Lexington Road
Louisville, Kentucky 40280

© The Andrew Fuller Center for Baptist Studies 2022

All rights reserved. No part of this publication may be reproduced, stored in a retrieval system, or transmitted, in any form or by any means, without the prior permission in writing of The Andrew Fuller Center for Baptist Studies, or as expressly permitted by law, by license, or under terms agreed with the appropriate reproduction rights organization.

ISBN 978-1-77484-062-7

Printed by H&E Publishing, Peterborough, Ontario, Canada

The Journal of Andrew Fuller Studies

The *Journal of Andrew Fuller Studies* is an open access, double-blind peer-reviewed, scholarly journal published online biannually in February and September by the Andrew Fuller Center for Baptist Studies (under the auspices of The Southern Baptist Theological Seminary). The publication language of the journal is English. Articles that deal with the life, ministry, and thought of the Baptist pastor-theologian Andrew Fuller are very welcome, as well as essays on his friends, his Particular Baptist community in the long eighteenth century (1680s-1830s), and the global impact of his thought, known as "Fullerism."

Articles and book reviews are to follow generally the style of Kate L. Turabian, *A Manual for Writers of Research Papers, Theses, and Dissertations*, 9th ed. (Chicago: University of Chicago Press, 2018). They may be submitted in British, American, Australian, New Zealand, or Canadian English. Articles should be between 5,000 and 8,000 words, excluding footnotes. Articles are to be sent to the Editor and book reviews to the Book Review Editors.

Editor:
Michael A G Haykin, ThD, FRHistS
Chair & Professor of Church History
& Director, The Andrew Fuller Center for Baptist Studies
The Southern Baptist Theological Seminary, Louisville, Kentucky
mhaykin@sbts.edu

Associate editors:
Ian Hugh Clary, PhD
Assistant Professor of Historical Theology
Colorado Christian University, Lakewood, Colorado
iclary@ccu.edu

Baiyu Andrew Song, PhD cand.
Assistant Professor of General Education Studies
Heritage College and Seminary
Cambridge, Ontario
bsong@heritagecs.edu

Design editor:
Dustin W. Benge, PhD
Associate Professor of Biblical Spirituality and Historical Theology
& Vice President of Communications
The Southern Baptist Theological Seminary, Louisville, Kentucky

Book review editors:
Josiah Michael Claassen, PhD cand.
The Southern Baptist Theological Seminary, Louisville, Kentucky
jclaassen800@students.sbts.edu

C. Anthony Neel, PhD cand.
The Southern Baptist Theological Seminary, Louisville, Kentucky
cneel914@students.sbts.edu

Editorial board:
Cindy Aalders, DPhil
Director of the John Richard Allison Library
& Assistant Professor of the History of Christianity
Regent College, Vancouver

Dustin Benge, PhD
Associate Professor of Biblical Spirituality and Historical Theology
& Vice President of Communications
The Southern Baptist Theological Seminary, Louisville, Kentucky

Dustin B. Bruce, PhD
Dean & Assistant Professor of Christian Theology and Church History
Boyce College, Louisville, Kentucky

Chris W. Crocker, PhD
Pastor, Markdale Baptist Church, ON
& Associate Professor of Church History
Toronto Baptist Seminary, Toronto, Ontario

Chris Chun, PhD
Professor of Church History & Director of the Jonathan Edwards Center
Gateway Seminary, Ontario, California

Jenny-Lyn de Klerk, PhD
Editor, Book Division
Crossway, Wheaton, Illinois

Jason G. Duesing, PhD
Provost & Professor of Historical Theology
Midwestern Baptist Theological Seminary, Kansas City, Missouri

Nathan A. Finn, PhD
Provost & Dean of the University Faculty
North Greenville University, Tigerville, South Carolina

C. Ryan Griffith, PhD
Pastor, Cities Church, St. Paul, Minnesota

Peter Morden PhD
Senior Pastor/Team Leader, Cornerstone Baptist Church
Leeds, England
& Distinguished Visiting Scholar
Spurgeon's College, London, England

Adriaan C. Neele, PhD
Director, Doctoral Program & Professor of Historical Theology
Puritan Reformed Theological Seminary, Grand Rapids, Michigan
& Research Scholar
Yale University, Jonathan Edwards Center, New Haven, Connecticut

Robert Strivens, PhD
Pastor, Bradford on Avon Baptist Church (UK)
& Lecturer in Church History
London Seminary, London, England

Tom Nettles, PhD
Senior Professor of Historical Theology
The Southern Baptist Theological Seminary, Louisville, Kentucky

Blair Waddell, PhD
Pastor, Providence Baptist ChurchHuntsville, Alabama

Contents

The Journal of Andrew Fuller Studies
No. 4, February 2022

Editorial | 9
Michael A.G. Haykin

Articles
Wesley, Whitefield, and High Calvinism: | 11
Rethinking the Free Grace Controversy and the
Authorship of *Free Grace Indeed!*
Jonathan N. Cleland

"The oppressed Ethiopian": | 31
Olaudah Equiano as the voice of a silent people
Steele B. Wright

"A Union of Sentiments in Apostolical Doctrines": | 45
The catholicity of Andrew Fuller
Lon Graham

Texts & documents
Writing to George Whitefield: A letter from | 61
Anne Dutton on sinless perfection
ed. Michael A.G. Haykin

"You will scarcely need another intimate friend": | 65
A letter of James Hinton to his daughter, Ann, on her marriage
ed. Chance Faulkner

"Eminent piety, and ministerial ability": | 71
James Hinton to his son on pastoral ministry
ed. Chance Faulkner

Book reviews | 77

Editorial

Michael A.G. Haykin

Michael A.G. Haykin is Chair and Professor of Church History and Director, The Andrew Fuller Center for Baptist Studies at The Southern Baptist Theological Seminary, Louisville, Kentucky.

The subjects of race and racism have been both controversial and prominent in the academic world for quite a while now. Recent developments in the western world such as the launching of the 1619 Project by the New York Times and the emergence of the Black Lives Matter movement have ensured that they continue to be so. Inevitably such events force us to rethink questions that we have about the past and why certain people and events have been highlighted. Thus, in this issue of the journal of the Andrew Fuller Center, after Jon Cleland's fine study of the controversy between George Whitefield and John Wesley, Steele Wright looks at the life of Olaudah Equiano through the prism of his famous narrative *The Interesting Narrative of the Life of Olaudah Equiano, or Gustavus Vassa, the African*. He demonstrates the way that this work needs to be interpreted as a document that has been shaped primarily by Equiano's reading of the Bible. It is noteworthy that when Equiano visited Birmingham in the summer of 1790 to promote the above-mentioned book, Andrew Fuller's close friend Samuel Pearce publicly supported Equiano. The subject of our third article, by Lon Graham, is a key aspect of the life and thought of Andrew Fuller, namely his catholicity. This also has a bearing on the present day, which has seen significant discord not only in the larger sphere of Western society, but also in the church.

As usual, we have some primary source documents—on this occasion, Anne Dutton's defence of Whitefield in his quarrel with Wesley and two letters from James Hinton—and our book reviews. Permit me to draw attention to one book review, namely, that of Matthew Roe's self-published *Preaching Deliverance to the Captives: Particular Baptist Sermons on the Abolition of the Slave Trade* (2021). This is a tremendous collection of key sermons preached by Particular Baptists, all of whom would have been known to Andrew Fuller, against the iniquity of the slave trade and slavery. Some of these sermons have been long forgotten, but they had a deep impact in their day, and it is good to be reminded of how and why Baptists were involved in the public square.

Wesley, Whitefield, and High Calvinism: Rethinking the Free Grace Controversy and the Authorship of *Free Grace Indeed!*[1]

Jonathan N. Cleland

Jonathan N. Cleland is a PhD student at Knox College, Toronto School of Theology, University of Toronto, and an adjunct lecturer at Heritage College and Seminary, Cambridge, ON.

Introduction

Throughout his lifetime, John Wesley (1703–1791) was no stranger to debating Calvinism. One of his best-known tracts in this regard is *Free Grace*, written and published in 1739.[2] Here, it is Wesley's aim to show that "the grace or love of God, whence cometh our salvation, is free in all, and free for all."[3] This tract is a polemic against Calvinist views like particular atonement and predestination. And, perhaps most famously, this tract is known for causing division between him and his dear friend George Whitefield (1714–1770), a fellow English evangelical clergyman.[4] Contemporary Wesley scholars Albert Outler and Richard

---

[1] This article was originally composed as a term paper for the seminar "John Wesley: Catholic Evangelical," led by Prof. Victor Shepherd at Wycliffe College in winter 2020. A revised version was presented at the Evangelical Theological Society Ontario/Quebec Regional meeting on October 16, 2021, at Toronto Baptist Seminary, Toronto, Ontario. I am thankful for the friends who listened to me that day and asked questions to help crystalize my argument. I am also thankful to my friend Baiyu Andrew Song for looking over my research, offering me insights and resources, and encouraging me to seek its publication.

[2] John Wesley, *Free Grace: A Sermon Preach'd at Bristol* (Bristol: S. and F. Farley, 1739).

[3] Wesley, *Free Grace*, 5.

[4] To say that Wesley had no friends who were Calvinists is to overstep the issue. Along with his friendship with Whitefield, Wesley also had a relationship with Howell Harris (1714–1773), another Calvinistic Methodist. See James L. Schwenk, *Catholic Spirit: Wesley, Whitefield, and the Quest for Evangelical Unity in Eighteenth-Century British Methodism* (Plymouth: Scarecrow, 2008), 87–88.

Heitzenrater even count this tract as "the signal of a major schism" between the two.[5] However, some of the critiques that Wesley makes of Calvinism in *Free Grace* seems disconnected from what he knew of Whitefield's thought.

While both Whitefield and Wesley wrote several letters to each other privately, the dispute did not become public until after the publication of a tract entitled, *Free Grace Indeed! A Letter to the Reverend Mr. John Wesley, relating to his sermon against absolute election; published under the title of Free Grace*.[6] This tract has recently been written on in an article by Maddock, who points out the timeline for its publication. Maddock shows that this tract was published in London by an anonymous author in May 1740 and that this led Wesley to reprint his own *Free Grace*.[7] It was partly then in reaction to the reprint of Wesley's *Free Grace* that Whitefield was prompted to publish his own response.[8] Although some claim that Whitefield wrote this tract, Maddock has persuasively argued that its authorship most likely belongs to someone else.[9] Yet, before asking who might have authored *Free Grace Indeed!*, one must first ask why Wesley preached and published *Free Grace* in the first place.

In Joel Houston's recent monograph, he argues that Wesley used the "free grace controversy" to distance his branch of Methodism from the Calvinistic Methodism of Whitefield.[10] Houston emphasizes the doctrine of predestination as the key difference between the two. However, while Houston speaks of Wesley as writing against high Calvinism, he likewise puts Whitefield into this high-Calvinistic camp due to Whitefield's view of reprobation.[11] Although

---

[5] Albert C. Outler, and Richard P. Heitzenrater, "Free Grace: An Introductory Comment," in *John Wesley's Sermons: An Anthology* (Nashville, TN: Abingdon Press, 1991), 49.

[6] Although originally printed in 1740, the 1741 printing is the copy now most readily available. See anonymous, *Free Grace Indeed! A Letter to the Reverend Mr. John Wesley, Relating to His Sermon Against Absolute Election; Published under the Title of Free Grace* (London, 1741).

[7] See Ian J. Maddock, "Solving a Transatlantic Puzzle?: John Wesley, George Whitefield, and 'Free Grace' Indeed!," *Wesley and Methodist Studies* 8, no. 1 (2016): 8.

[8] Maddock, "Solving a Transatlantic Puzzle," 8–9. Different printings of Whitefield's response exist. For the one printed in 1741 in London, see George Whitefield, *A Letter to the Reverend Mr. John Wesley: In Answer to his Sermon, Entitled, Free-Grace* (London: W. Strahan, 1741).

[9] The view that Whitefield wrote this tract is held by Susan F. Harrington in "Friendship Under Fire: George Whitefield and John Wesley, 1739–1741," *Andover Newton Quarterly* 15, no. 3 (1975): 167–181. For example, in the conclusion Harrington offers the suggestion that "the document Whitefield mentioned in his letter of February 1 was Whitefield's tract 'Free Grace Indeed!'" (Harrington, "Friendship Under Fire," 181). On Maddock's argument, see Maddock, "Solving a Transatlantic Puzzle," 14.

[10] See Joel Houston, *Wesley, Whitefield, and the "Free Grace" Controversy: The Crucible of Methodism* (New York: Routledge, 2020), 99–124.

[11] See Houston, *Wesley, Whitefield, and the "Free Grace" Controversy*, 126, 138.

this article builds on Houston's premises in seeing Wesley's sermon polemically functioned for the purpose of placing his own branch of Methodism over and above Whitefield's, this article differs from Houston on the understanding of high Calvinism.[12] It is the aim of this article to show that some of the stronger claims in Wesley's tract are not best seen as an attack against evangelical Calvinism—as Whitefield's ministry and response makes clear—but rather against the high Calvinism of the nonconformists of his time.[13] So contrary to the un-

---

[12] A problem with Houston's view of high Calvinism is that he never actually defines the term. At times, he seems to use it interchangeably with hyper-Calvinism (see, for instance, Houston, *Wesley, Whitefield, and the "Free Grace" Controversy*, 73) and to base it on a view of supralapsarianism and reprobation. For example, Houston argues that "Beza's rigid doctrinal parsing and emphasis on the supralapsarian scheme gave rise to extreme forms of Calvinistic soteriology ('hyper-Calvinism')" (Houston, *Wesley, Whitefield, and the "Free Grace" Controversy*, 42). However, in speaking about Whitefield, although he considers him a high Calvinist, he mentions that Whitefield seems to have identified himself as holding to infralapsarianism (Houston, *Wesley, Whitefield, and the "Free Grace" Controversy*, 140). Moreover, he speaks elsewhere of Wesley writing against a "hyper-Calvinist position that Whitefield did not hold" (Houston, *Wesley, Whitefield, and the "Free Grace" Controversy*, 142). These seemingly varied uses of these terms create a large degree of uncertainty concerning what Houston means by "high Calvinism" and "hyper-Calvinism" and in what areas he would see differentiation between "hyper-Calvinism," "high Calvinism," and "evangelical Calvinism."

Despite what Houston means exactly by his use of the term "high Calvinism," it can be seen from history that the views of supralapsarianism or reprobation do not of necessity lead to the high Calvinistic practices that were prevalent in the 18th century. Although Houston aims to situate the "free grace controversy" within the history of predestination (for example, see Houston, *Wesley, Whitefield, and the "Free Grace" Controversy*, 19–66), he nevertheless seems to conflate the views of supralapsarianism and reprobation with the practice of high Calvinism, while lacking sufficient historical evidence. Many supralapsarians, including the oft-accused Theodore Beza (1519–1605), did not succumb to many of the problems shown in the practice of high Calvinists in the 18th century (for a contemporary and accessible defence of Beza, see Shawn D. Wright, *Theodore Beza: The Man and the Myth* [Fearn, Scotland: Christian Focus Publications, 2015]). Although one could say that supralapsarianism *can* lead to high Calvinistic practice, it is historically unwarranted to say that it *must*. Moreover, it can likewise be possible that one can be an infralapsarian and a high Calvinist, as was the case for John Brine and John Gill. For this point, see David Rathel, "A Pastor-Theologian in Search of a Faith Worthy of All Acceptation: The Theological Genealogy of Andrew Fuller and His Critique of It" (PhD diss., University of St Andrews, 2018), 3–4.

In this article, I will look to rectify the problems created by Houston's undefined view of high Calvinism by situating Whitefield and Wesley within the high Calvinistic thought that was amongst the English nonconformists. In order to do this, I am indebted to the research of Peter Toon, *The Emergence of Hyper-Calvinism in English Nonconformity 1689–1765* (1967; repr., Eugene, OR: Wipf & Stock, 2011). Although Toon uses the term "hyper-Calvinism," the doctrinal issues are the same as "high Calvinism," which is my preferred term.

For the use of the term "high Calvinism" in the place of "hyper-Calvinism," as well as the history and understanding of the terms of "high Calvinism" and "evangelical Calvinism" leading up to the nineteenth-century, see Ian J. Shaw, "The Development of High and Evangelical Calvinism to c. 1860," in *High Calvinists in Action: Calvinism and the City: Manchester and London, c. 1810–1860* (New York: Oxford University Press, 2002), 10–36.

[13] For a very brief comparison of Whitefield's Calvinism with the high-Calvinistic thought of his time, see Sean McGever, *Born Again: The Evangelical Theology of Conversion in John Wesley and George Whitefield*, Studies in Historical and Systematic Theology (Bellingham, WA: Lexham Press, 2020), 103–104.

derstanding of high Calvinism being based on a certain view of predestination, as is presented by Houston, this article understands high Calvinism as the view held by those who denied the free-offer of grace in preaching and advocated a perspective that could lead to practical antinomianism.[14]

Thus, to compliment Houston's argument, it could be understood that Wesley used the high-Calvinistic milieu familiar in his time to attack Whitefield, and to subsequently present his own branch of Methodism in a more positive light.[15] In doing so, Wesley separated Whitefield's Calvinistic Methodism from the theological tradition of the Established Church; instead, Wesley placed Calvinism into a theological camp that was consistent with nonconformism. In practice, Whitefield was careful to use the writings of John Edwards (1637–1716), who was a Calvinist clergyman in the Church of England.[16] For Whitefield desired to hold together both Calvinism and the Anglican tradition.[17] By using the high Calvinism of some nonconformists to confront Whitefield's Calvinism, Wesley condemned Whitefield's soteriology and ecclesiology, as the former showed that Whitefield's Calvinism could lead not only to perverse practices, but also that such practices associated Calvinistic Methodists with those outside of the Anglican Communion.

While Irwin Reist argues that Wesley at times had "a gross misunderstanding of Whitefield's Calvinism," and David Ceri Jones mentions that Wesley "had mistakenly assumed that Calvinism was a monochrome theological system, that all Calvinists were uniformly committed to strict double predestination," this article presents the potential view that Wesley was aware of the unfair

---

[14] On these being distinctives of high Calvinism, see Shaw, "The Development of High and Evangelical Calvinism to c. 1860," 11. Notice here also that these views are not necessarily based on supralapsarianism, but on doctrines such as eternal justification and eternal sanctification.

[15] In dialogue with Allan Coppedge, *John Wesley in Theological Debate* (Wilmore, KY: Wesley Heritage Press, 1987), Houston points to the possibility that Wesley was using the thought of John Gill (1691–1771) in his preaching of *Free Grace*. Houston writes, "Lastly, it actually serves the argument that Wesley was attempting to wrest control of the Methodist societies in Bristol by preaching against the worst possible configuration of predestination instead of seeking harmony with Whitefield" (Houston, *Wesley, Whitefield, and the "Free Grace" Controversy*, 126). Although Houston makes this point, he does not expand on it, nor does he display how Whitefield's evangelical Calvinism is different from Gill's high Calvinism. Moreover, as I hope to show, Gill cannot be the only high Calvinist Wesley had in mind, even if he was a major leader of the movement. Thus, it is my aim to further elaborate on this idea of Wesley using high Calvinism, and in doing so, I hope to provide clarity regarding the differences between Whitefield's Calvinism and the high Calvinism of his time.

[16] On Edwards as a Calvinist and a conformist, see Dewey D. Wallace, Jr., *Shapers of English Calvinism, 1660–1714: Variety, Persistence, and Transformation* (New York, NY: Oxford University Press, 2011), 205–242.

[17] On Whitefield's potential use of Edwards for the reason of holding Calvinism and the Established Church in harmony, see Houston, *Wesley, Whitefield, and the "Free Grace" Controversy*, 143–145.

picture he was presenting of Whitefield's Calvinism and that he was doing so intentionally for the sake of better endorsing his own branch of Methodism over against that of Whitefield's.[18]

In order to show the disparity between the critique of Whitefield with what Wesley actually knew of Whitfield, this article will survey two of the critiques that Wesley makes against Calvinism before showing how these do not fit with what Wesley knew of Whitefield's thought and practice. Instead, I will present select high Calvinists to show how the ideas presented in some of these documents communicate the issue that Wesley is writing against. In this way, it can be speculated that Wesley's intent in *Free Grace* is to use the high Calvinism of his time to critique Whitefield for the sake of a greater divide between his branch of Methodism and that of Whitefield's. In conclusion, keeping with the view that Wesley is most directly writing against high Calvinism, I will then aim to build on Maddock's work by looking at the tract *Free Grace Indeed!* and by asking if the writer of this document could have been a high Calvinist who felt attacked by Wesley's tract.

Free Grace, *Whitefield, and high Calvinism*
In *Free Grace*, Wesley follows his introduction with the claim that grace "is free in all to whom it is given."[19] From here, Wesley moves into the topic of predestination, the doctrine that before creation God saved some and damned others, and then into how this doctrine leads to the denouncing of key Christian practices. While Wesley mentions eight points in total,[20] two deserve specific attention as they point to the potential that Wesley uses the thought of others apart from Whitefield for the sake of his argument—namely, those who are now referred to as high Calvinists. As Hammond notes: "Wesley's sermon *Free Grace*, targeted at the doctrine of reprobation, expressed his fears of the consequences of Calvinist doctrine rather than the content of what we know of Whitefield's teaching."[21] These consequences, however, while irrelevant to the practice of Whitefield, are evident in the teaching of select high Calvinists in Wesley's period and location. Thus, in this section, I will raise two corollaries that Wesley

---

[18] Irwin W. Reist, "John Wesley and George Whitefield: A Study in the Integrity of Two Theologies of Grace," *Evangelical Quarterly* 47, no. 1 (March 1975): 35; David Ceri Jones, "George Whitefield and the Revival of Calvinism in Eighteenth-Century Britain," *International Congregational Journal* 14, no. 1 (2015): 109.

[19] Wesley, *Free Grace*, 5.

[20] On the eight points and Whitefield's eventual response to them, see Houston, *Wesley, Whitefield, and the "Free Grace" Controversy*, 125–160; Reist, "John Wesley and George Whitefield," 35–38.

[21] Geordan Hammond, "Whitefield, John Wesley, and Revival Leadership," in *George Whitefield: Life, Context, and Legacy*, eds. Geordan Hammond and David Ceri Jones (New York: Oxford University Press, 2016), 112.

believes predestination will lead to, showing how these do not fit with Whitefield's practice or the beliefs as he expressed them in his response letter. Instead, I will argue that these corollaries point to the teaching of high Calvinism and are used by Wesley for the sake of condemning Whitefield's Methodism and aiming to equate him with those outside the Church of England.

Preaching and the offer of grace
The first corollary Wesley points out is that predestination makes "all preaching vain."[22] Whether a person is preached to or not does not change whether a person is elect or not. And so, Wesley argues, predestination claims that a person will either be saved or damned regardless of another's actions and thus preaching is not needed.[23] It is questionable, though, if Wesley's critique can rightly be levelled against Whitefield.

In February of the same year that *Free Grace* was published, Whitefield gave in to his conviction and preached in the field for the first time.[24] Notably, it was Wesley who followed Whitefield in this ministry, as he began field-preaching a month later.[25] It was in April that Wesley drew lots and received the conviction to "preach and print" his sermon *Free Grace*.[26] This means that the preaching and subsequent publishing of *Free Grace* came only months after Whitefield and Wesley began field-preaching. It seems quite unlikely that Wesley would attack Whitefield by arguing how the latter's theology led to the belief that preaching was useless to the non-elect.[27]

In Whitefield's letter, written in response to Wesley, he argues that preaching is a means by which God brings his people to salvation.[28] Such preaching is to be done for all people without discrimination, and God will use it as he will to

---

[22] Wesley, *Free Grace*, 10.

[23] Wesley, *Free Grace*, 10.

[24] Ian J. Maddock, *Men of One Book: A Comparison of Two Methodist Preachers, John Wesley and George Whitefield* (Eugene, OR: Wipf & Stock, 2011), 40.

[25] Maddock, *Men of One Book*, 56.

[26] Outler and Heitzenrater, "Free Grace: An Introductory Comment," 49. See also John Wesley's letter to James Hutton on April 30, 1739, http://wesley.nnu.edu/john-wesley/the-letters-of-john-wesley/wesleys-letters-1739/ (accessed on January 30, 2022).

[27] On Whitefield encouraging Wesley to preach outdoors, see Hammond, "Whitefield, John Wesley, and Revival Leadership," 106; Maddock, *Men of One Book*, 36.

[28] George Whitefield, *A Letter From the Reverend Mr. George Whitefield, To the Reverend Mr. John Wefley, in Answer To His Sermon, Entitled 'Free Grace'* (Boston, MA: G. Rogers, 1740), 12. Although it was also printed in London in 1741, the American version is the most accessible and hence is cited in this article.

save those whom he has elected.[29] Whitefield's response to Wesley, along with his ministry of evangelistic preaching, displays how Wesley's claim that Calvinism presents preaching as vain would not be warranted if directed toward Whitefield. However, his argument would make sense if Wesley was using the high Calvinism of his time, which his readers would have been familiar with, to make his point.

An example of this high-Calvinistic denial of a free offer of grace in preaching can be found in the teaching of Joseph Hussey (1660–1726), an English Congregationalist, who had "a strategic position in the creation of Hyper-Calvinism in England."[30] In Hussey's *God's Operations of Grace but No Offers of His Grace*, he makes the following statement:

> Men do likewise urge that the said Free Grace and *full Salvation* is propounded, Tendred, *Offer'd* and Preached, and ought so to be, *to all Sinners within the Sound*. They make the Tender of *Salvation* it self for Acceptance to *all* that they may be *saved*. And this also they call Preaching the Gospel. Howbeit this Conceit, in such as profess against the Notion of a General Redemption, doth bring them in … *Self-Condemned*.[31]

According to Hussey, free grace is not to be offered to all, but to the elect alone.[32] One of his key reasons was that offering grace and salvation to sinners will not be of any aid, as God alone is the one who saves an individual.[33] To be sure, such preaching that does not offer the gospel to all is deserving of the critique made by Wesley and seems to fit with the teachings of high Calvinists like Hussey.

Although some of Hussey's books were limited in printed copies, their impact was nevertheless significant.[34] For instance, Hussey impacted the thought of John Skepp (1675–1721), who later influenced John Gill (1691–1771).[35] In fact, as David Rathel states, "John Skepp served as Gill's personal mentor and

---

[29] Whitefield, *Letter*, 12.

[30] Toon, *Emergence of Hyper-Calvinism in English Nonconformity*, 70.

[31] Joseph Hussey, *God's Operations of Grace but No Offers of His Grace. To which are added, Two brief Treatises. The One about Invitation, and the other about Exhortation of Sinners to come to Christ; Both examin'd, and consistently Stated with the Glory of Free Grace: to rectify some Common and Prevailing Mistakes in Ministers, who now, with Time, are running on in the Present Generation* (London: D. Bridge, 1707), 10.

[32] Toon, *Emergence of Hyper-Calvinism in English Nonconformity*, 79.

[33] Toon, *Emergence of Hyper-Calvinism in English Nonconformity*, 80.

[34] Toon, *Emergence of Hyper-Calvinism in English Nonconformity*, 84.

[35] Toon, *Emergence of Hyper-Calvinism in English Nonconformity*, 85.

preached Gill's instalment service at his church in London."[36] Thus, through the writing of Hussey, passed on by the thought of Skepp, Gill and others became influenced by the high-Calvinistic view of non-offer grace.[37] Despite claims to the contrary, Rathel argues that "Gill indeed denied Gospel offers and duty faith."[38] Gill, according to Rathel, "believed that universal offers of grace are insincere, both on the part of ministers who make the offers and, ultimately, on the part of God."[39]

In sum, it seems that Wesley would have in mind high Calvinists, such as John Gill, when he accuses Whitefield of the same errors, knowing in practice that Whitefield does not align with them. While Whitefield holds preaching as a means of grace for all, the high Calvinists hold that the elect alone can be saved regardless. In this way, the first corollary of predestination is shown in the practice of the high Calvinists and is potentially being used by Wesley to confront the Calvinism of Whitefield for the sake of creating a negative association between Whitefield's Calvinistic Methodism and the practice of the high Calvinists.

Holiness and free-will

The second corollary of holding predestination, according to Wesley, is "that it directly tends to destroy that holiness, which is the end of all the ordinances of God."[40] For Wesley, if a person is set to go either to heaven or to hell solely based on predestination, then the primary motive for holiness—"the hope of future reward and fear of punishment, the hope of heaven and fear of hell"—is no longer relevant.[41]

Although Sean McGever mentions that there are several theological differences between Wesley and Whitefield, he argues that "they had much overlap regarding the theology of conversion."[42] Conversion for Whitefield was

[36] David Mark Rathel, "John Gill and the History of Redemption as Mere Shadow," *Journal of Reformed Theology* 11, no. 4 (2017): 381.

[37] Toon, *Emergence of Hyper-Calvinism in English Nonconformity*, 88–89.

[38] David Mark Rathel, "Was John Gill a Hyper-Calvinist? Determining Gill's Theological Identity," *Baptist Quarterly* 48, no. 1 (January 2017): 48.

[39] Rathel, "Was John Gill a Hyper-Calvinist," 52.

[40] Wesley, *Free Grace*, 11.

[41] Wesley, *Free Grace*, 11. Along very similar lines is corollary four, the tendency for predestination to kill the zeal to do good works (Wesley, *Free Grace*, 16). Much of what is said in this section can also be said for that point. In Whitefield's letter, he even passes over this point, claiming that what he says in response to the second corollary is sufficient (See Whitefield, *Letter*, 23).

[42] Sean McGever, "The Vector of Salvation: The New Birth as (Only) the Beginning of Conversion for Wesley and Whitefield," in *Wesley and Whitefield? Wesley Versus Whitefield?*, ed. Ian J. Maddock (Eugene,

to be progressive throughout a believer's life, marked "by the forsaking of sin through repentance, bringing forth fruit in godly living, and generally going beyond general civility toward actual godliness."[43] This teaching is evident in Whitefield's sermon, *The Conversion of Zaccheus*, published originally in 1739.[44] Here, speaking of Zaccheus receiving Christ by faith in his heart, he makes the comment, "Say not any of you within yourselves, this is a licentious, Antinomian doctrine; for this faith, if true, will work by love, and be productive, of the fruits of holiness," something seen in the way good works are evident in Zaccheus after his conversion.[45]

Along with his sermon on Zaccheus, Wesley and Whitefield had also worked together in February 1739 to publish *An Abstract of the Life and Death of the Reverend Learned and Pious Mr. Tho. Halyburton, M.A.* in which both men presented the conversion and holy life of Scottish divine Thomas Halyburton (1674–1712) as a spiritual model.[46] With a sermon that affirmed the importance of holiness and a joint publication in which they promoted a life of holiness as a model for believers, it seems unfair that only months later Wesley would critique Whitefield as holding a theology which has the opportunity to destroy the pursuit of holiness.

In his letter, Whitefield responds to Wesley's attack on how the Calvinist doctrine tends to destroy holiness and mentions that a Christian should seek

---

OR: Pickwick Publications, 2018), 37. In his monograph, McGever expands on his argument that there are many similarities between Wesley and Whitfield's theology of conversion and presents "nine synoptic espoused statements" that are shared by both of them to argue this (McGever, *Born Again*, 2). They both, according to McGever, share a view of conversion that can be termed "inaugurated teleology," where the emphasis is "on the *telos* of salvation rather than the *arché* of salvation" (McGever, *Born Again*, 13). Thus, McGever argues that, for both Wesley and Whitefield, conversion is only the beginning of the Christian life, one that is to grow into a life of holiness.

[43] McGever, "The Vector of Salvation," 38.

[44] McGever, "The Vector of Salvation," 39.

[45] George Whitefield, "The Conversion of Zaccheus," in *Ten Sermons on the Following Subjects; viz, I. Christ, the Believer's Husband. II. The Gospel Supper. III. Blind Bartimeus. IV. Walking with God. V. The Resurrection of Lazarus. VI. Britain's Mercies and Britain's duty. VII. Christ, the Believer's Wisdom, Righteousness, Sanctification, and Redemption. VIII. The Pharisee and Publican. IX. The Holy Spirit Convincing the World of Sin, Righteousness, and Judgment. X. The Conversion of Zaccheus* (Glasgow: W. Mitchell and J. Knox, 1751), 177. Although originally published in 1739, this copy of the sermon is most readily available.

[46] Hammond, "Whitefield, John Wesley, and Revival Leadership," 105. Hammond also points out that, although they did work together on this project, Wesley included in the preface a note about the possibility of having freedom from sin, a matter that Whitefield was very upset with. In fact, Whitefield would later publicly disown Wesley's view of sinless perfection (see Hammond, "Whitefield, John Wesley, and Revival Leadership," 105). For an interesting letter by Anne Dutton to George Whitefield on the view of sinless perfection, see Anne Dutton, "Writing to George Whitefield: A Letter from Anne Dutton on Sinless Perfection," ed. Michael A.G. Haykin, *Southern Baptist Journal of Theology* 18, no. 2 (2014): 83–86.

holiness out of love and gratitude for Christ, regardless of desire for reward or fear of punishment.[47] Moreover, the desire for rewards continues to be a motive, for, Whitefield poses, even amongst the elect, do they not "know that the more good works they do, the greater will be their reward?"[48] Thus, Whitefield's sermon, his similar conviction and joint publication with Wesley, and points in his letter all display that Wesley's condemnation of Calvinism's debilitation of holiness cannot be applied to Whitefield or his kind of Calvinism. Instead, it seems that the target is better pointed at the antinomian practice of certain high Calvinists.

To illustrate how such practical Antinomianism would later corrode certain churches, one can look to the famous account that took place in England roughly 30 years after the "free grace controversy." This account from 1770 concerns the newly baptized Andrew Fuller (1754–1815) of being informed of a member at his church—James Levit—who had a drinking problem.[49] However, when Fuller confronted him, Levit responded with the fact that he was not able to stop, and that it was not even his fault as he was not ultimately his own. When Fuller told his pastor John Eve (d. 1782) about the matter, the pastor agreed with Fuller that the man should refrain from sinning, and subsequently took the issue before select members of the church. When he did so, the general consensus was that a person could not keep oneself from evil, and while they were to be blamed for their own conduct, if one restrained from this sin or gave in to it, such things were ultimately to be attributed to God rather than the individual. Here, thirty years after the "free grace controversy," one reads of a clear example of how high Calvinism not only destroyed holiness but ultimately allowed for sin in an individual's life as it was viewed as a matter of God's ordination.

But was this same doctrine prevalent before and during the time of Wesley's ministry? In his exposition of Wesley's doctrine of Christian perfection, Shepherd argues that, for Wesley to claim that God does not deliver one from all sin is the equivalent to saying that one must sin. And to imply this is to excuse and undermine human responsibility.[50] Shepherd then makes the following parenthetical comment: "Here Wesley has in mind such thinkers as John Gill, a contemporary whose hyper-Calvinism Wesley deplored not least because it

---

[47] Whitefield, *Letter*, 13.

[48] Whitefield, *Letter*, 13.

[49] The following account is a summary from Andrew Gunton Fuller, *Andrew Fuller* (London: Hodder and Stoughton, 1882), 32–33. For more on this account, see also E.F. Clipsham, "Andrew Fuller and Fullerism: A Study in Evangelical Calvinism," *Baptist Quarterly* 20, no. 3 (1963): 107.

[50] Victor A. Shepherd, *Mercy Immense and Free: Essays on Wesley and Wesleyan Theology*, rev. ed. (Toronto: BPS, 2016), 103.

appeared to render God the author of sin."[51] If Shepherd is right, then what Wesley saw in Gill is the same passivity to sin as the young Fuller saw at his church.

John Wesley and John Gill were no strangers to each other. Although it is very likely that they were both familiar with the other's ministry and thought, a formal and public dispute came about between them in 1752 over the doctrine of predestination and final perseverance.[52] Concerning the former, Wesley published *Predestination Calmly Considered*, in which he "makes it plain that his complaint is not merely doctrinal, but practical: he fears that those who hold to predestination will, because they consider themselves elect, lapse into Antinomianism and loose living."[53] For example, in this sermon, Wesley comments that those who believe that Christ died for them and therefore will be saved regardless might say to themselves, "if I am one of the elect, I must and shall be saved. Therefore I may safely sin a little longer; for my salvation cannot fail."[54] Furthermore, Wesley goes on to say that the doctrine of predestination has a natural and genuine tendency "to prevent or obstruct holiness."[55] Although this tract is published thirteen years after the "free grace controversy," one can see that the general concern for holiness and how Calvinism might diminish it is handled by Wesley in the same way. The question to address is whether Wesley read Gill correctly and, if so, was this his teaching more than thirteen years earlier; for, if this was the case, then Gill may have been in Wesley's mind while writing *Free Grace*.

Notably, Gill was charged on several occasions by Abraham Taylor (fl. 1727–1740) with the claim that he was an antinomian.[56] This led Gill to publish three tracts, one in 1732, another in 1736, and a final one in 1739.[57] In the tract published in 1739, *Necessity of Good Works unto Salvation Considered*, Gill

---

[51] Shepherd, *Mercy Immense and Free*, 103.

[52] For the debate over final perseverance of the saints, see Alan P.F. Sell, David J. Hall, and Ian Sellers, eds., *Protestant Nonconformist Texts: Volume 2* (2006, Eugene, OR: Wipf & Stock, 2015), 130–133.

[53] Sell, Hall, Sellers, eds., *Protestant Nonconformist Texts*, 128.

[54] John Wesley, "Predestination Calmly Considered," *The Arminian Magazine* 2 (December 1779): 633–634. However, Gill's *The Doctrine of Grace cleared from the Charge of Licentiousness* (1737) looks to deny this claim. For more on this, see Curt Daniel, "John Gill and Calvinistic Antinomianism," in *The Life and Thought of John Gill (1697–1771): A Tercentennial Appreciation*, ed. Michael A.G. Haykin (Leiden: Brill, 1997), 181.

[55] Wesley, *Predestination Calmly Considered*, 634.

[56] On this account, see G.M. Ella, "John Gill and the Charge of Hyper-Calvinism," *Baptist Quarterly* 36, no. 4 (1995): 170–171.

[57] See Toon, *Emergence of Hyper-Calvinism in English Nonconformity*, 98.

emphasizes that salvation is to come from Christ alone and not by any works.[58] For, if good works of any kind are necessary, then that means that all infants who die are doomed. But, in the case that salvation comes from Christ alone and not by works, then "parents may hope for the salvation of their infants."[59] Yet while works are not necessary for salvation in one sense, they are still to be done by those who are saved by Christ, on account of God's will.[60] Gill writes, "They are necessary to adorn the doctrine of God our Saviour, to recommend religion to others, to testify the truth of our faith, and give evidence of the reality of internal holiness."[61] In this way, works are both necessary in one sense, and yet not so in another.[62] With such a view, Wesley would have been hard-pressed to charge Gill with a claim of anti-holiness in 1739 in the same way he would attempt to charge Whitefield.[63] Yet perhaps a connecting key might be found in Gill's mentor, John Skepp.

Skepp, who was influenced by Joseph Hussey, only wrote one treatise that was published posthumously in 1722--a year after his death.[64] Skepp's *Divine Energy* could potentially pair with Wesley's concerns and the later practice found in some churches like Soham. In his 1722 treatise, Skepp emphasizes that holiness apart from the Spirit is not true holiness. On the contrary, "You must first have the Spirit of Holiness to make you holy within, or you never will be holy, except in outward Shew."[65] Thus, one must not promote sanctification without the Spirit. Moreover, "Sanctification is a passive Work wrought upon

---

[58] John Gill, *The Necessity of Good Works unto Salvation Considered: Occasion'd by some Reflections and Misrepresentations of Mr. (alias Dr.) Abraham Taylor, in a Pamphlet of his lately published, called, An Address to young Students in Divinity, by way of Caution against some Paradoxes, which lead to Doctrinal Antinomianism* (London: A. Ward, 1739), 17.

[59] Gill, *Necessity of Good Works unto Salvation Considered*, 18.

[60] Gill, *Necessity of Good Works unto Salvation Considered*, 10.

[61] Gill, *Necessity of Good Works unto Salvation Considered*, 11.

[62] See Daniel, "John Gill and Calvinistic Antinomianism," 182.

[63] A question, of course, is whether Gill actually practiced what he wrote. It may have been that Wesley's perception of Gill may have been different from what he here states, but in writing at least, it seems like, in 1739, Gill had at least some sense of the importance of holiness in his thought.

[64] See Toon, *Emergence of Hyper-Calvinism in English Nonconformity*, 85.

[65] John Skepp, *Divine Energy: or the Efficacious Operations of the Spirit of God upon the Soul of Man, in his Effectual Calling and Conversion, Stated, Prov'd and Vindicated. Wherein the Real Weakness and Insufficiency of Moral Suasion. (Without the Supereddition of the exceeding Greatness of God's Power,) for Faith, and Conversion to God, are fully envivced. Being an Antidote against the Pelagian Plague* (London: Joseph Marshall, 1722), 203.

us; it is God the Spirit sanctifies."[66] With these statements in mind, Skepp seems to be concerned that one did not call a sinner to do something that they are unable to do, namely, accept the Gospel and avoid sin. Furthermore, he was even concerned, it seems, to exhort a saved person to strive after holiness, as such holiness comes passively from the Spirit alone.[67] This perception of holiness may have led to a passivity in pastors not calling out their parishioners to live in a godly way as this was something accomplished by the Spirit alone. It may be, then, that this concept from Skepp could have been something that Wesley feared and wrote against. Although this work of Skepp was produced in 1722, his thought had a long-lasting influence. As Toon writes, "Skepp stands, as it were, in the history of dogma, as the connecting link between Hussey's theology and the Hyper-Calvinism of many Particular Baptists throughout the eighteenth century."[68]

Conclusively, then, Wesley's critique that Calvinism would lead to a denouncement of holiness is not warranted as being directed against Whitefield, nor is it even warranted against Gill in light of his 1739 publication. Rather, it seems possible that Wesley again uses the high Calvinist thought, in this case evidenced by people like Skepp, to attack Whitefield. This shows that the critique Wesley is making must go beyond the high Calvinism of just Gill to encompass the greater high Calvinistic thought practiced in his time.

An objection

At this point, an objection could be made. Although it is true that Wesley is unfairly critiquing what he knew of Whitefield's Calvinism at the time of writing, one could ask if Wesley genuinely believed Calvinism would lead to the dangers that he wrote about. Especially seeing that *Free Grace* was written relatively early in his theological career, it could be that Wesley believed that all who held to Calvinist teaching would end up eventually succumbing to the same logical conclusions as those held by the high Calvinists.

In partial defense of such an argument, one could appeal to Wesley's view of Martin Luther (1483–1546) around this time. Even though both Luther and the Moravians had positive impacts on Wesley early on, in 1741 he would pair the teaching of Luther in his *Galatians Commentary* with the thought of the Moravians that he would come to take issue with.[69] One of the key concerns Wesley had with the Moravians was their rejection of the importance of good

---

[66] Skepp, *Divine Energy*, 203.

[67] Also see Toon, *Emergence of Hyper-Calvinism in English Nonconformity*, 87–88.

[68] Toon, *Emergence of Hyper-Calvinism in English Nonconformity*, 88–89.

[69] See Leo G. Cox, "John Wesley's View of Martin Luther," *Bulletin of the Evangelical Theological Society* 7, no. 3 (1964): 86–88.

works and supposedly found Luther "speaking blasphemously" about them in his commentary.[70] On Wesley's connection of the Moravians with Luther, Cox writes, "Wesley was looking at one thing, namely, Moravian errors. His quick scan of this commentary found the seeds of their errors."[71] It is generous to argue that Wesley simply did not read carefully and comprehensively enough of Luther at this time to know of Luther's robust theology of holiness.[72] Moreover, his contextual reading in light of his break with the Moravians made it hard for him to read Luther objectively. If so, could it not be that Wesley's presentation of Whitefield's Calvinism was likewise simplistic and without awareness of the diverse forms of how Calvinism was lived out?

Right away, an issue with this view would be raised concerning Wesley's reading of history. In the summer of 1741, Wesley found himself in the Bodleian Library reflecting on the case between John Calvin (1509–1564) and Michael Servetus (d. 1553), about which Wesley read in one of Calvin's works.[73] In his reflection, Wesley is aware of the conflict and he views Calvin as being unfair toward Servetus. Notably, this account does not present Wesley as a novice of Calvin's works or thought; instead, it alludes to the fact that Wesley was familiar with the writings of Calvin and knew of his ministry. Thus, it could be asked: could Wesley not see that Calvin's predestinarian views did not, in fact, lead him to eventually stop preaching? Or that his stance on holiness was not retracted over time? How could Wesley believe that his warning of evangelical Calvinism would inevitably lead to high Calvinism? Based on his awareness of history, he must have known that not all those who held to predestination subsequently diminished preaching and holiness. Subsequently, Wesley could not have simply been naïve.[74]

Based on a letter Wesley sent to Whitefield in 1741, it seems impossible to suggest that Wesley was merely offering a warning to Calvinists to avoid high Calvinism. In this letter, which was sent after the publication of Whitefield's

---

[70] Cox, "John Wesley's View of Martin Luther," 87.

[71] Cox, "John Wesley's View of Martin Luther," 87.

[72] See Cox, "John Wesley's View of Martin Luther," 87. For a recent study of Luther's theology of holiness, see Phil Anderas, *Renovatio: Martin Luther's Augustinian Theology of Sin, Grace and Holiness* (Göttingen: Vandenhoeck & Ruprecht, 2019).

[73] John Wesley, Journal for Thursday, July 9, 1741 in *The Works of John Wesley: Journal and Diaries II (1738-1743)*, Vol. 19, ed. by W. Reginald Ward & Richard P. Heitzenrater (Nashville, TN: Abingdon Press, 1990), 204.

[74] And even if he was somehow naïve, if he truly wanted to present a cogent case against Calvinism, he would have first needed to study those who held to predestination in the past. In doing this, he would have seen the robust theology of preaching and holiness held by many of the predestinarians throughout their ministries.

response to *Free Grace*, Wesley confronts Whitefield on misrepresenting his position. Wesley is very dismissive of Whitefield's letter, and, in return, Wesley states that he will deal with Whitefield in the same way that he has been dealt with. Therefore, Wesley resolves to "publicly repeat all the wrong expressions which I have heard from Predestinarians."[75] Notice that Wesley does not resolve to repeat only the wrong expressions he has seen in a certain expression of predestinarians, such as in the thought of Whitefield; rather, Wesley resolves to repeat *all* wrong expressions that he has witnessed from the predestinarians. It seems that Wesley has knowingly and purposefully conflated the views of all Calvinistic practices that he is aware of into one in order that "all that heard me would run from a Predestinarian as they would from a mad dog."[76] His goal does not seem to be to deter people simply from one group of predestinarians, but from all of them. Wesley's tract is viewed by him at this point then not as a warning against high Calvinism, but as a complete dismissal of all Calvinistic thoughts. Thus, it seems that Wesley's interest is not to issue a doctrinal warning; instead, he sees it as necessary for all Calvinists to amend their views.

Furthermore, when Charles Wesley wrote to his brother in fall of 1741, the former mentioned to John that "Whitefield preaches holiness very strongly, and free grace to all; yet at the same time he uses expressions which necessarily imply reprobation."[77] But Whitefield does this, according to Charles, "in order to convey the poison more successfully."[78] It is thus evident that Charles knew John was unfairly critiquing Whitefield on these two points; yet, he never reprimanded him for doing so. Instead, he seems to imply that his brother should critique Calvinism by any means in order to eradicate the poison. From this letter, John Wesley would have known without a doubt that he was unfairly critiquing Whitefield; nevertheless, he did not recant his views. To the contrary, he upheld the foreign views that he placed onto Whitefield. In the same way that Wesley seemingly read the Moravian errors into Luther's theology of holiness, he seems to have imposed the high Calvinist errors onto Whitefield's evangelical Calvinism.

---

[75] Letter from John Wesley to George Whitefield, London, April 27, 1741, http://wesley.nnu.edu/john-wesley/the-letters-of-john-wesley/wesleys-letters-1741/ (accessed on January 30, 2022).

[76] Letter from John Wesley to George Whitefield, London, April 27, 1741, http://wesley.nnu.edu/john-wesley/the-letters-of-john-wesley/wesleys-letters-1741/ (accessed on January 30, 2022).

[77] Letter from Charles Wesley to John Wesley, fall, 1741, as introduced and cited in Houston, *Wesley, Whitefield, and the "Free Grace" Controversy*, 116–117.

[78] Letter from Charles Wesley to John Wesley, fall, 1741, as introduced and cited in Houston, *Wesley, Whitefield, and the "Free Grace" Controversy*, 116–117.

Rethinking the authorship of Free Grace Indeed!
Shortly after having preached his sermon on *Free Grace*, Wesley makes an interesting entry in his journal. On Wednesday, May 2, he comments that he was at Newgate when the following took place: "I was desired to stop thence to a neighbouring house to see a letter wrote against me, as 'a deceiver of the people', by teaching that God 'willeth *all men* to be saved.'"[79] This account is interesting as it seems to be one of the earliest responses to Wesley's *Free Grace* sermon. Could it be that the person who wrote this note was John Gill who ministered nearby in Southwark? Or perhaps Gill's mentee, the high Calvinist John Brine (1703–1765) who ministered in Cripplegate?[80] Although the editors of Wesley's journal do not comment on who the author of this letter might be, it is interesting to see how quickly there was a response to his sermon. It seems at least possible that whoever wrote this letter could have also been connected to the person who wrote the tract, *Free Grace Indeed!*

Having argued that at least two of the critiques of Wesley point to the thought of high Calvinism rather than the Calvinism of Whitefield, the remaining part of this article examines the document *Free Grace Indeed!* to see if there may be new insight into the authorship of this tract.

As mentioned, it was the publication of *Free Grace Indeed!* in 1740 that led Wesley to the reprinting of his tract *Free Grace*. Before the publication of *Free Grace Indeed!* Whitefield and Wesley had an agreement that Wesley would not reprint *Free Grace*. Nevertheless, with the publication of *Free Grace Indeed!* Wesley included an advertisement in his 1740 edition of *Free Grace* which mentioned his decision to terminate the agreement and subsequently to reprint the tract.[81] It was only after this reprinting that Whitefield would then print his letter in response.[82] The beginning of this public debate, then, really was in part initiated by the anonymously penned *Free Grace Indeed!* After this publication, there was a clear and overt public debate between Wesley and Whitefield. Before it, the discussions were done only privately in letters.[83] Speculating that Wesley used the high Calvinism of his time to confront Whitefield's branch of Methodism, could it be that, feeling most threatened, the high Calvinists were in fact the first ones to respond publicly to Wesley's tract?

---

[79] John Wesley, Journal for Wednesday, May 2, 1739, in *Works of John Wesley*, 19:53.

[80] For a study on John Brine, see Peter Beck, "John Brine 1703–1765," in *The British Particular Baptists*, ed. Michael A.G. Haykin and Terry Wolever (Springfield, MO: Particular Baptist Press, 2018), 4:210–235.

[81] Maddock, "Solving a Transatlantic Puzzle?," 8.

[82] Maddock, "Solving a Transatlantic Puzzle?," 9.

[83] For a recent and brief overview of the private exchanges, see Houston, *Wesley, Whitefield, and the "Free Grace" Controversy*, 107–112.

It is quickly evident that the responses offered in Whitefield's letter are more persuasive and thorough than the ones offered in *Free Grace Indeed!* For example, in the latter, the author does not offer a satisfying response to the second corollary that Wesley offers on holiness, as the author's response is at best a question, "How come you to know this?"[84] All in all, the author does not offer a helpful response to Wesley's objection regarding holiness, and it may be due to a lack of concern on the part of the author who may not see the importance of the topic.[85]

In regard to preaching, the author responds that election still holds, so that a person may preach and there is subsequently no danger in doing so. Further, the author comments that the means are decreed just as the end is.[86] Again, the response is far less nuanced than the one offered by Whitefield, as the author does not fully address the critique. Moreover, the author speaks about preaching, but not about an offer of grace. It could be that the brief reply is similar to the high Calvinistic link to preaching to all, yet not offering grace to all—a nuance that would be seemingly difficult to maintain.[87]

Could it be, then, that the critique by Wesley in *Free Grace* was first publicly responded to for the first time by someone within the high Calvinist community? It seems at the least plausible. However, more research needs to be done to determine what theology the author of *Free Grace Indeed!* held to, along with the literary clues it may give to the authorship. But one thing is certain; based on the timeline and the differences in the cogency and thoughtfulness of responses to Wesley's claim, the author of *Free Grace Indeed!* is indeed someone other than Whitefield.[88]

Conclusion

In this article, I have surveyed the potential that Wesley penned *Free Grace* with the framework of high Calvinism so as to unfairly create a greater divide between his camp of Methodism and the Calvinistic Methodism of Whitefield. In this way, I have looked to build on the thesis of the recent monograph by Houston. However, I have also modified Houston's argument by giving a definition and exposition of the thought and practice of the high Calvinism potentially being used by Wesley in contrast to the evangelical Calvinism of Whitefield. If

---

[84] Anonymous, *Free Grace Indeed!*, 20.

[85] See Anonymous, *Free Grace Indeed!*, 19–21.

[86] Anonymous, *Free Grace Indeed!*, 19.

[87] For this view in the thought of Hussey, see Toon, *Emergence of Hyper-Calvinism in English Nonconformity*, 80–83.

[88] Again, as is in agreement with Maddock, "Solving a Transatlantic Puzzle," 1–15.

Wesley did indeed purposefully use the thought of high Calvinism in his *Free Grace* sermon, then he did so not only to falsely critique Whitefield's view of Calvinism, but also to place him in harmony with those outside of the Church of England that Whitefield so desperately wanted to be a part of. Further, I have also aimed to build on the research of Maddock's article by opening the possibility of *Free Grace Indeed!* having been written by a high Calvinist who felt directly targeted by Wesley. This presents the possibility for further study into the question of the authorship of this anonymous yet crucial tract.

"The oppressed Ethiopian": Olaudah Equiano as the voice of a silent people

Steele B. Wright

Steele B. Wright is a PhD student in Christian Preaching at The Southern Baptist Theological Seminary. His research is focused on the preaching of Andrew Fuller. Currently, Steele and his wife, Brooke, reside in Knoxville, TN, where Steele serves as a Pastor at Lonsdale Community Church.

In March of 1788, Queen Charlotte, the wife of the British monarch George III, received an appeal that urged her to exercise compassion on the millions of Africans who languished under the hand of tyranny in the West Indies.[1] The letter read, in part: "I presume, therefore, gracious Queen, to implore your interposition with your royal consort, in favour of the wretched Africans; that, by your Majesty's benevolent influence, a period may now be put to their misery; and that they may be raised from the condition of brutes, to which they are at present degraded, to the rights and situation of men."[2] The author continued his fervent petition to the Queen and expressed gratitude for her benevolent reign before concluding: "I am your Majesty's most dutiful and devoted servant to command, Gustavus Vassa, The oppressed Ethiopian."[3]

That an African, who was once a slave, could appeal to the Queen on behalf of his people is remarkable and it reveals something of the significance of this letter's author. Born Olaudah Equiano (1745–1797), he was renamed Gustavus

---

[1] Olaudah Equiano, *The Interesting Narrative and Other Writings*, ed. Vincent Carretta, rev. ed. (New York: Penguin Books, 2003), 231.

[2] Equiano, *Narrative*, 231–232.

[3] Equiano, *Narrative*, 232.

Vassa by his master, Michael Henry Pascal, while traveling from Virginia to England in 1754.[4] Gustavus Vasa, or Gustavus I (1496–1560) of Sweden, was familiar to many in Britain at the time as the subject of a well-known play, *Gustavus Vasa, the Deliverer of his Country*, which depicted the Swedish ruler who freed his people from Danish oppression in 1523.[5] While the irony of his new name might have been lost on the young Equiano, he later came to see it as an indelible mark of the Lord's providence in his life.

Intentionally giving voice to a silent multitude, Equiano described himself as "the oppressed Ethiopian."[6] The meaning behind this unique title lay not in its geographical connection to Equiano's origins—given that he traced his roots to the Igbo region of West Africa and not Ethiopia—but in its biblical significance.[7] Equiano drew a direct line from himself to the Ethiopian eunuch in Acts 8, who was the first African to believe in Christ, a sign that the message of the gospel was indeed universal and impartial.[8] By identifying himself as a brother in Christ, oppressed by those who claimed the same Savior, Equiano strengthened his apologetic appeal and assumed his place as a leading African voice in the abolitionist cause that would eventually result in the freedom of his people.

Equiano first introduced himself to the English-speaking world through his autobiography, *The Interesting Narrative of the Life of Olaudah Equiano, or Gustavus Vassa, the African. Written by Himself*, which went through an astounding nine editions during his lifetime.[9] Written as part spiritual autobiography and

---

[4] Equiano, *Narrative*, 64. For further explanation, see Vincent Carretta, *Equiano, the African: Biography of a Self-Made Man* (Athens, GA: University of Georgia Press, 2005), 42. In this essay, I will use his given name, Olaudah Equiano.

[5] Equiano, *Narrative*, 252.

[6] Henry Louis Gates, Jr. observes how Equiano's *Narrative*, "was considered to epitomize the sufferings of millions of silent slaves held captive throughout the South" (*The Classic Slave Narratives* [New York, NY: Signet Classics, 2002], 1–2).

[7] The question of Equiano's origins has sparked significant debate in recent years. The traditional understanding is that Equiano was born in the Igbo region of Nigeria, as he stated in his autobiography and maintained throughout his life. Carretta offers a revised position in his critical biography, arguing that Equiano was probably born in South Carolina, as his baptismal and naval records indicate. See Carretta, *Equiano*. While this debate falls outside the scope of the present work, I accept the traditional understanding of Equiano's origins. For a defense of this view, see Paul E. Lovejoy, "Autobiography and Memory: Gustavus Vassa, alias Olaudah Equiano, the African," *Slavery & Abolition* 27.3 (2006): 317–347.

[8] For an illuminating study of Equiano's use of the book of Acts as a tool for his abolitionist work, see Hannah Wakefield, "Olaudah Equiano's Ecclesial World," *Early American Literature* 55.3 (2020): 651–683.

[9] Carretta remarks, "Thanks largely to profits from his publications, when Equiano died on 31 March 1797 he was probably the wealthiest and certainly the most famous person of African descent in the Atlantic world" (*Equiano*, xii).

part slave narrative, Equiano designed this work with the hope that "it may still be the means, in its measure, of showing the enormous cruelties practiced on my sable brethren, and strengthening the generous emulation now prevailing in this country, to put a speedy end to a traffic both cruel and unjust."[10] The *Narrative*'s subscribers included many prominent figures ranging from members of the royal family to influential abolitionists such as Granville Sharp to the father of Methodism, John Wesley, who was reading a copy of Equiano's work just before his death in 1791.[11]

Much of the modern scholarship on Equiano's life tends to focus on his roles as a former slave, political activist, and savvy businessman, who by the time of his death was one of the wealthiest Africans in all of England.[12] But to place any of these at the center of Equiano's life is to obscure who he believed himself to be; namely, one who "saw clearly, with the eye of faith, the crucified Saviour" and who knew "what it was to be born again."[13] When read through this distinctly Christian lens, the meta-narrative of Equiano's book is understandable and three distinct themes emerge. First, Equiano embraced the biblical narrative as the prime interpreter of his own experience, both as an individual and as a member of the larger African population. Second, he understood his sufferings to be the outworking of God's good providential plan for his life. Finally, he used the story of his life and his own conversion to craft a firm yet winsome apologetic against one of the great evils of his day.

---

[10] Equiano, *Narrative*, 5. For an assessment of Equiano's *Narrative* as spiritual autobiography, see Adam Potkay, "Olaudah Equiano and the Art of Spiritual Autobiography," *Eighteenth-Century Studies* 27.4 (1994): 677–692. Paul E. Lovejoy proposes the description "freedom narrative" as an alternative for the traditional "slave narrative," given that Equiano's greatest achievements came through gaining his freedom and the work he accomplished as a free man. See his "'Freedom Narratives' of Transatlantic Slavery," *Slavery & Abolition* 32.1 (2011): 91–107.

[11] For complete list of the subscribers, see Equiano, *Narrative*, 15–28. On Wesley, see Carretta, "Introduction," in Equiano, *Narrative*, xxix.

[12] On Equiano's skill in self-promotion, see Carretta, "A Self-Made Man," in *Equiano*, 330–368. Frederiks goes so far as to argue that Equiano's "religious representations mainly serve abolitionist ends," implying that Equiano's spiritual life was a means to a greater end. This interpretation, while favorable to a modern secular audience, ultimately does not account for Equiano's profound spiritual struggle and born-again experience that altered the course of his life. That Equiano's conversion contributed to his work as an abolitionist is clear, but to suggest he doctored his own religious experience for the sake of his political aspirations is to move beyond what the primary source material indicates. See Martha T. Frederiks, "Olaudah Equiano's Views of Europe and European Christianity," *Exchange* 42.2 (2013): 175–197.

[13] Equiano, *Narrative*, 190.

Embodying the Biblical narrative

> Well may I say my life has been
> One scene of sorrow and of pain;
> From early days I griefs have known,
> And as I grew my griefs have grown.
>
> Dangers were always in my path,
> And fear of wrath and sometimes death;
> While pale dejection in me reign'd,
> I often wept, by grief constran'd.
>
> When taken from my native land,
> By an unjust and cruel band,
> How did uncommon dread prevail!
> My sighs no more I could conceal.[14]

On the opening page of his *Narrative*, Equiano humbly addressed his readers, "I offer here the history of neither a saint, a hero, nor a tyrant."[15] Indeed, Equiano's life began quietly enough in the year 1745 when he was born in "a charming and fruitful vale, named Essaka" in Igbo, West Africa.[16] As he recalled the early days among his own people, Equiano described their life as a tranquil and dignified existence, one of simple luxuries, abundant harvests, and a "necessary habit of decency" that manifested itself in his people's careful attention to personal hygiene and religious purifications.[17] In addition to these ritual cleansings was a shared a belief in "one Creator of all things" and an observance of the rite of circumcision.[18] After carefully recounting the details of his childhood, Equiano concluded, "I cannot forbear suggesting what has long

---

[14] Following his conversion, Equiano wrote a hymnic reflection of his life, entitled "Miscellaneous Verses; Or, Reflections on the State of my Mind during my first Convictions of the Necessity of believing the Truth, and of experiencing the inestimable Benefits of Christianity." See Equiano, *Narrative*, 194.

[15] Equiano, *Narrative*, 31.

[16] Equiano, *Narrative*, 32. Lovejoy believes Equiano was born in 1742, meaning he purchased his freedom at 24, rather than 21. See Paul E. Lovejoy, "Equiano's World" (Lecture 1 in the W.E.B. Dubois Lecture Series at Harvard University, Cambridge, Massachusetts, April 16–18, 2019).

[17] Equiano, *Narrative*, 41. Though Equiano largely described a simple and quiet early life, slavery and war were common occurrences. However, the slavery he described among his fellow Africans stood in stark contrast to his later experiences in colonial slavery. See Paul E. Lovejoy, *Transformations in Slavery: A History of Slavery in Africa*, 3rd ed. (New York: Cambridge University Press, 2012).

[18] Equiano, *Narrative*, 40–41.

struck me very forcibly, namely, the strong analogy which even by this sketch, imperfect as it is, appears to prevail in the manners and customs of my countrymen, and those of the Jews."[19]

When Equiano was kidnapped at eleven years old and carried to the western Atlantic shore over a span of several months, he vividly recalled how his conditions worsened as he approached the coastal hub of his European captors, where he was "hurried away even among the uncircumcised."[20] Intentionally evoking the biblical language often directed towards Israel's oppressors, Equiano identified his European captors with the enemies of God. In no uncertain terms, he observed, "the white people looked and acted, as I thought, in so savage a manner; for I had never seen among any people such instances of brutal cruelty."[21] Equiano described the scenes on the Middle Passage from Africa to the Caribbean in further horrifying detail before questioning his readers, "O, ye nominal Christians! might not an African ask you, learned you this from your God? who says unto you, Do unto all men as you should men should do unto you?"[22] The tension Equiano saw between the professed faith of his captors and the cruelty he experienced at their hands only contributed to his grief, even as he began to call out to their God for himself:

"Sighs now no more would be confin'd
They breath'd the trouble of my mind:"
I wish'd for death, but check'd the word,
And often pray'd unto the Lord.

Unhappy, more than some on earth,
I thought the place that gave me birth—
Strange thoughts oppress'd—while I replied,
"Why not in Ethiopia died?"

And why thus spar'd, when nigh to hell!—
God only knew—I could not tell!—
"A tott'ring fence, a bowing wall,
I thought myself e'er since the fall."

Oft times I mus'd, and nigh despair,

---

[19] Equiano, *Narrative*, 43.

[20] Equiano, *Narrative*, 53.

[21] Equiano, *Narrative*, 57.

[22] Equiano, *Narrative*, 61.

While birds melodious fill'd the air.
"Thrice happy songsters, ever free,"
How blest were they compar'd to me![23]

Equiano's Edenic descent from blissful freedom to this unholy captivity took him to a place of profound despair, one in which he often wished "for the last friend, Death, to relieve me."[24] In time, Equiano's situation steadily improved as he came under the authority of a new master, Michael Henry Pascal, who was a lieutenant in the royal navy and commander of a trading ship.[25] It was Pascal who later renamed him and afforded Equiano the opportunity to learn to read and write. Though his fall from innocence was great, Equiano acknowledged, "I could very plainly trace the hand of God, without whose permission a sparrow cannot fall. I began to raise my fear from man to him alone, and to call daily on his holy name with fear and reverence."[26]

As Equiano grew older, his journeys at sea continued, and he slowly began to appropriate not only the corporate experience of God's people to that of his countrymen, but also the individual experiences of God's chosen servants to that of his own.[27] Having purchased his freedom in 1766, Equiano experienced a renewed optimism about his future. Nevertheless, his subsequent journeys were not without their own perils. In February of 1767, while on passage to Georgia, Equiano dreamed that "the ship was wrecked amidst the surfs and rocks, and that I was the means of saving every one on board."[28] Soon after, Equiano's ship was caught in a storm and sustained significant damage as it was

---

[23] Equiano, *Narrative*, 195.

[24] Equiano, *Narrative*, 56.

[25] Equiano, *Narrative*, 63.

[26] Equiano, *Narrative*, 88.

[27] For an extensive look at Equiano's use of the Bible, see R.S. Sugirtharajah, "An Emancipator as Emancipator of Texts: Olaudah Equiano and His Textual Allusions," in *The Bible and the Third World: Precolonial, Colonial and Postcolonial Encounters* (Cambridge: Cambridge University Press, 2001), 75–87. Sugirtharajah comments "the stories of the Bible offered him the potential for understanding his life, and he used them as a weapon to oppose the very institution of slavery which had denied him his humanity" (*Bible and the Third World*, 77). Sugirtharajah overstates his case at times, arguing that Equiano "unhinged" the Bible from its original context to serve his own purposes, a practice that he claims was unique among Protestant Christians at the time (*Bible and the Third World*, 87). By appropriating the Biblical narrative to fit his own experience, Equiano may not have conformed to later modernist understandings of biblical interpretation, but neither was he doing something that was foreign to his readers. One finds a striking similarity between Equiano's use of the Bible and that of his evangelical contemporaries, and the Puritans a century before them. Viewing one's own experience through the lens of Scripture has been an integral part of Christian interpretation throughout the centuries.

[28] Equiano, *Narrative*, 148.

thrown violently against the rocks.[29] As he watched several of his fellow sailors calm their fears with incessant drinking, Equiano busied himself by repairing the ship and rowing swiftly to safety. "Had we not worked in this manner," he reflected, "I really believe the people could not have been saved; for not one of the white men did any thing to preserve their lives; and indeed they soon got so drunk that they were not able, but lay about the deck like swine, so that we were at last obliged to lift them into the boat, and carry them on shore by force."[30] Like the Apostle Paul, Equiano was a lowly traveler whom God chose as the appointed means of saving the lives of those aboard his ship.[31] His words following the near-disastrous encounter echo those of the apostle in Acts 27:25: "But these things did not deter me; I said, "Let us again face the winds and seas, and swear not, but trust to God, and he will deliver us."[32] Just as Paul made it his ambition to stand before Caesar to advocate for his release, so too would Equiano, sharing a similar motivation, one day stand before the powers-that-be of his own day to advocate for the freedom of his people.

Suffering under the hand of Providence

> Weary with troubles, yet unknown
> To all but God and self alone,
> Numerous months for peace I strove,
> Numerous foes I had to prove.
>
> Inur'd to dangers, grief, and woes,
> Train'd up 'midst perils, death, and foes,
> I said, "Must it thus ever be?
> No quiet is permitted me."
>
> Hard hap, and more than heavy lot!
> I pray'd to God, "Forget me not—
> What thou ordain'st help me to bear;
> But, O! deliver from despair!"[33]

Now a free man, Equiano's physical condition steadily improved even as his

---

[29] Equiano, *Narrative*, 149.

[30] Equiano, *Narrative*, 151.

[31] See Acts 27:1–44.

[32] Equiano, *Narrative*, 158.

[33] Equiano, *Narrative*, 196.

spiritual condition continued to deteriorate. Although he was baptized into the Church of England in 1759 at St. Margaret's in Westminster, he admitted, "I was determined to work out my own salvation, and, in so doing, procure a title to heaven."[34] His frequent brushes with death only reminded him of the uncertainty surrounding the state of his soul. With a testimony of conversion that mirrored many of his evangelical contemporaries, Equiano wrestled with God for months and found precious little comfort through his spiritual exercises. "I had the fears of death hourly upon me," he confessed, "and shuddered at the thought of meeting the grim king of terrors in the natural state I then was in, and was exceedingly doubtful of a happy eternity if I should die in it."[35] Although he worked as hard as any to secure his freedom from slavery, he could not, by the same token, free himself from the chains of his own spiritual bondage.

Even as he struggled, Equiano recalled how from early years he was "a predestinarian," who learned early in life to "look at the hand of God in the minutest occurrence, and to learn from it a lesson of morality and religion."[36] Indeed, Equiano referred to the hand of providence no less than two dozen times throughout his *Narrative*, most often as it related to God's careful preservation of his life, his freedom from slavery, and his eventual conversion. It was this same hand that permitted him no rest until he was "brought to a stand, not knowing which to believe, whether salvation by works, or by faith only in Christ."[37] Again finding his place alongside the saints of old, Equiano reflected, "It pleased God to enable me to wrestle with him, as Jacob did: I prayed that if sudden death were to happen, and I perished, it might be at Christ's feet."[38]

At Christ's feet he did soon fall, though not in death, but in faith. In 1774, a dissenting evangelical minister invited Equiano to attend a love feast at his chapel. When his guest arrived, he was surprised "to see the place filled with people, and no signs of eating and drinking."[39] As the meeting wore on, Equiano observed, "there were many ministers in the company. At last they

[34] Equiano, *Narrative*, 178.

[35] Equiano, *Narrative*, 175. Equiano's frequent encounters with death bear a striking similarity to John Newton's account of his spiritual struggles and subsequent conversion on the high seas. See Newton's *Authentic Narrative of Some Remarkable and Interesting Particulars in the Life of* —— (N.p., 1764), which recounts the story of Newton's early years and conversion.

[36] Equiano, *Narrative*, 119. This reflection occurs in the final paragraph of the *Narrative*, in which Equiano continued, "and in this light every circumstance I have related was to me of importance" (Equiano, *Narrative*, 236).

[37] Equiano, *Narrative*, 186.

[38] Equiano, *Narrative*, 189.

[39] Equiano, *Narrative*, 183.

began by giving out hymns, and between the singing, the ministers engaged in prayer."[40] Not knowing what to make of the scene, Equiano was confused even as he admired a "kind of Christian fellowship I had never seen, nor ever thought of seeing on earth."[41] Though new to this particular expression of godly community, this was not Equiano's first encounter with the blossoming evangelical movement. In February of 1765, Equiano made his way into a crowded church in Savannah, Georgia to hear a "pious man exhorting the people with the greatest fervour and earnestness."[42] This man, he soon learned, was George Whitefield, who was on his sixth visit to the American colonies at the time.[43]

Now, nine years had passed, and Equiano's senses were reawakened to the realities of the new birth, the forgiveness of sins in Christ, and the assurance that follows. Soon after this meeting, Equiano opened his Bible to Acts 4:12 and read the text with new eyes, "Neither is there salvation in any other: for there is none other name under heaven given among men, whereby we must be saved." Upon seeing the truth of this verse, Equiano vividly recalled, "the Lord was pleased to break in upon my soul with his bright beams of heavenly light; and in an instant, as it were, removing the veil, and letting light into a dark place. I clearly saw, with the eye of faith, the crucified Saviour bleeding on the cross on Mount Calvary."[44] Just as the Lord had sovereignly worked to preserve him "midst perils, death, and foes," Equiano understood his salvation to be the fruit of a similar kind of work. Thus, in looking back on this experience alongside many others, he concluded, "I regard myself as a particular favourite of Heaven, and acknowledge the mercies of Providence in every occurrence of my life."[45]

Slavery and the heart of man

> Like some poor pris'ner at the bar,
> Conscious of guilt, of sin, and fear,
> Arraign'd, and self-condemn'd, I stood,
> "Lost in the world and in my blood!"

---

[40] Equiano, *Narrative*, 183.

[41] Equiano, *Narrative*, 184.

[42] Equiano, *Narrative*, 132.

[43] In his biography, Equiano states that he heard Whitefield in Philadelphia in 1766. However, Whitefield was in Britain during this time. Carretta traces Equiano's encounter with Whitefield to February, 1765, a time at which both Whitefield and Equiano were both in Savannah, Georgia. See Equiano, *Narrative*, 277.

[44] Equiano, *Narrative*, 190. The portrait of Equiano that forms a frontispiece, as it were, to this article, depicts Equiano holding the Scriptures open to Acts 4:12.

[45] Equiano, *Narrative*, 31.

> Yet here, 'midst blackest clouds confin'd,
> A beam from Christ, the day-star, shin'd;
> Surely, thought I, if Jesus please,
> He can at once sign my release.
>
> Thus light came in, and I believ'd;
> Myself forgot, and help receiv'd!
> My Saviour then I know I found,
> For, eas'd from guilt, no more I groan'd.[46]

In time, Equiano connected the implications of his conversion to the ongoing plight of his countrymen. He, "like some poor pris'ner at the bar" had come beneath the mercy of Christ, who did "at once sign my release."[47] Equiano continued in the seafaring business for some time following his conversion, but he soon became disgusted with the whole affair, particularly as he witnessed the ongoing mistreatment of those still suffering under the yoke of slavery. In March of 1787, Equiano received his dismissal from the Navy. "From that period to the present time," he later recalled, "my life has passed in an even tenor, and great part of my study and attention has been to assist in the cause of my much injured countrymen."[48] Nothing would assist the cause of his countrymen more than the publishing of his *Narrative*, which propelled him to the forefront of the abolitionist cause.

The power of Equiano's anti-slavery argument in his *Narrative* is a product of both the horrors he witnessed first-hand and the vivid language he used to rouse a sleeping British conscience.[49] His unique ability to critique and to commend his British audience is evident from the opening pages:

> By the horrors of that trade I was first torn away from all the tender connexions that were dear to my heart; but these, through the mysterious ways of Providence, I ought to regard as infinitely more than compensated by the introduction I have thence obtained to the knowledge of the Christian religion, and of a nation which, by its liberal sentiments, its humanity, the glorious freedom of its government, and its proficiency in

---

[46] Equiano, *Narrative*, 196–197.

[47] Equiano, *Narrative*, 196.

[48] Equiano, *Narrative*, 231.

[49] For an interesting study on Equiano and eighteenth-century views on African identity from both the pro-slavery and the anti-slavery position, see George E. Boulukos, "Olaudah Equiano and the Eighteenth-Century Debate on Africa," *Eighteenth-Century Studies* 40.2 (2007): 241–255.

arts and sciences, has exalted the dignity of human nature.[50]

In this short statement, Equiano wisely placed himself and his British audience on the side of human dignity over and against the barbarity of the slave trade. When understood as allies in this great cause, they could both now mount an attack on their common enemy.

Equiano's *Narrative* established a pattern for later anti-slavery arguments, both in England in the early decades of the nineteenth century and in the United States some fifty years later.[51] The famed American abolitionist and former slave, Frederick Douglass (1817–1895), adopted the same spirit in a speech given in Rochester, New York on July 5, 1852, entitled, "The Meaning of July Fourth for the Negro." Douglass designed his words to pierce the American conscience by exposing their own hypocrisy; "You boast of your love of liberty, your superior civilization, and your pure Christianity, while the whole political power of the nation is solemnly pledged to support and perpetuate the enslavement of three million of your countrymen ... You are all on fire at the mention of liberty for France and Ireland; but are as cold as an iceberg at the thought of liberty for the enslaved of America."[52] The apologetic tactic used by Douglass, and Equiano before him, called those with the power to overturn the slave trade to simply live according to the stated principles of their governments and the professed values of their religion.

As a fellow Christian, Equiano skillfully spoke the language of Scripture to his British contemporaries. The book of Acts, a favorite for Equiano, was particularly useful for his anti-slavery arguments as he sought to establish a common humanity between his African kin and their British captors. Citing Acts 17:26, which speaks of the God "who hath made of one blood all nations of men for to dwell on all the face of the earth" (KJV), Equiano reminded his readers that reflecting on this truth should "melt the pride of their superiority into sympathy for the wants and miseries of their sable brethren, and compel them to acknowledge, that understanding is not confined to feature or colour."[53] By elevating the dignity of Africans alongside that of his British audience, Equiano was now prepared to offer perhaps his strongest critique of slavery: that it brutalized both the slave and the master.

---

[50] Equiano, *Narrative*, 7.

[51] Carretta writes of Equiano's *Narrative*, "It is universally accepted as the fundamental text in the genre of the slave narrative" (Equiano, *Narrative*, xii).

[52] Frederick Douglass, "The Meaning of July Fourth for the Negro, speech at Rochester, New York, July 5, 1852," in *Frederick Douglass, Selected Speeches and Writings*, ed. Philip S. Foner (Chicago, IL: Lawrence Hill Books), 1999, 202–203.

[53] Equiano, *Narrative*, 45.

Equiano reserved his harshest critiques for places like the West Indies, which was notorious for the poor treatment of its slaves.[54] Commenting on the cruelty of a law that required a single payment of fifteen pounds as compensation for the murder of a slave, Equiano charged his readers, "Do not the assembly which enacted it, deserve the appellation of savages and brutes rather than of Christians and men?"[55] He continued, "Is not the slave trade entirely at war with the heart of man? And surely that which is begun, by breaking down the barriers of virtue, involves in its continuance destruction to every principle, and buries all sentiments in ruin!"[56] Not only were slaves suffering at the hands of cruel masters, but also the very fabric of British society was threatened by the continued existence of an enterprise that undermined her cherished principles of virtue and liberty. Equiano traced this situation to its logical end:

> Such a tendency has the slave-trade to debauch men's minds, and harden them to every feeling of humanity! … Surely this traffic cannot be good, which spreads like a pestilence, and taints what it touches! Which violates the first natural right of mankind, equality and independency, and gives one man dominion over his fellows which God could never intend![57]

The use of such penetrating insights into the nature of humanity combined with Equiano's own personal experience to produce a work that reverberated throughout the British Empire. Reflecting on his childhood memories of being taken from his native home and placed into forced subjugation, Equiano succinctly concluded, "To me life had lost its relish when liberty was gone."[58] Prior to his conversion, Equiano frequently longed for his departure from this world. Despite not knowing what awaited him on the other side, he still "called upon God's thunder, and his avenging power, to direct the stroke of death to me, rather than permit me to become a slave, and to be sold from lord to lord."[59]

---

[54] Kenneth Morgan identifies both the harsh conditions of the sugar plantations in the West Indies and the cruel treatment of slaves by their masters as two reasons why this region was particularly infamous. In later decades, abolitionists understandably targeted the West Indies in their anti-slavery campaign. See Kenneth Morgan, *Slavery and the British Empire: From Africa to America* (Oxford: Oxford University Press), 2007.

[55] Equiano, *Narrative*, 109.

[56] Equiano, *Narrative*, 110.

[57] Equiano, *Narrative*, 111.

[58] Equiano, *Narrative*, 120.

[59] Equiano, *Narrative*, 98.

Mercifully, on every occasion, Equiano's life was spared and experiences such as these were later used as kindling for the fire of his abolitionist work.

Conclusion

After his conversion, Equiano recalled a distinct change in his approach to the subject of death; "Now my whole wish was to be dissolved, and to be with Christ—but, alas! I must wait my appointed time."[60] On March 31, 1797, Equiano reached his appointed time, ten years before Parliament's decision to abolish the slave trade in the British Empire. Even as he passed from this life, Equiano's voice echoed throughout subsequent decades. Reflecting on the power of his *Narrative* in the mid-nineteenth century, later abolitionist authors commended Equiano's account to a new generation: "Reading it we may well confess that truth is 'stranger than fiction;' and we ought to confess too that this black brother of ours was manifestly as much the object of God's providential care, as the most gifted and powerful of human beings. Yes, this child of a despised race, and a dark skin, he too had a soul to be cared for, and to be saved."[61]

---

[60] Equiano, *Narrative*, 193.

[61] F.W. Chesson and Wilson Armistead, "Chapter V. Biographical Sketches. Olaudah Equiano," in *God's Image in Ebony: Being a Series of Biographical Sketches, Facts, Anecdotes, etc., Demonstrative of the Mental Powers and Intellectual Capacities of the Negro Race*, ed. H.G. Adams (London: Partridge and Oakey, 1854), 73.

Today, Equiano's work has been made accessible to the public through online projects in the United States and the United Kingdom. See "Equiano's World" (http://equianosworld.org) led by Paul Lovejoy, and "Olaudah Equiano" (https://equiano.uk).

"A Union of Sentiments in Apostolical Doctrines": The catholicity of Andrew Fuller[1]

Lon Graham

Lon Graham (PhD, Vrije Universiteit Amsterdam) is the pastor of The Woods Baptist Church in Tyler, TX.

Introduction

The concept of catholicity has been understood in various ways throughout the centuries.[2] It is helpful, therefore, as a way of more fully exploring the concept, to focus on important thinkers and leaders in order to see how their thought and practice sheds light on the overall understanding of catholicity. This article describes the catholicity, or catholic spirit, of Andrew Fuller, a leading pastor and theologian among the English Particular Baptists in the late-eighteenth and early-nineteenth centuries.[3] At the outset, it is important to understand

---

[1] This article was originally published in *Journal of European Baptist Studies* 21.1 (2021): 105–122. Reprinted with permission.

[2] See Willem Van Vlaustin, *Catholic Today: A Reformed Conversation about Catholicity* (Göttingen: Vandenhoeck and Ruprecht, 2020), 18–161.

[3] There has been a resurgence of interest in Fuller in recent years. See, for example, Michael A.G. Haykin, *"At the Pure Fountain of Thy Word": Andrew Fuller as an Apologist* (Milton Keynes: Paternoster, 2004); Peter J. Morden, *The Life and Thought of Andrew Fuller, 1754–1815* (Milton Keynes: Paternoster, 2015); the Works of Andrew Fuller Project under the general editorship of Michael A.G. Haykin, published by Walter de Gruyter, which aims to publish critical editions of all of Fuller's works. For a more complete account of recent publications about Fuller, see Nathan A. Finn, "The Renaissance in Andrew Fuller Studies: A Bibliographic Essay," *Southern Baptist Journal of Theology* 17.2 (2013): 44–61.

that this article does not mean to engage with recent scholarship related to Baptist catholicity, but, rather, it aims to provide historical perspective on how one of the chief theologians of the Particular Baptists understood relations to those outside of his theological and denominational tradition.[4] It will focus on the language with which Fuller himself would have been familiar: the language of catholicity, or a catholic spirit.[5] Studying the catholicity of someone like Andrew Fuller is not a straightforward task, as he did not write a treatise which can be studied for a definition or theological foundation. This is not to say he thought it unimportant; he wrote shorter works about, and made important statements in longer works on a catholic spirit and adjacent topics. These must be studied collectively in order to understand his thought. Adding to the difficulty is the fact that there is some disagreement as to whether Fuller himself even possessed a catholic spirit. On the one hand, he is portrayed in one recent publication as catholic in sentiment because of his friendship with John Ryland, Jr. (1753–1825), who did not share Fuller's views on closed communion.[6] On the other hand, an earlier writer, John Buckley, pastor of the

---

[4] For more information on this, see Steven R. Harmon, *Towards Baptist Catholicity: Essays on Tradition and the Baptist Vision* (Eugene, OR: Wipf and Stock, 2006); Curtis W. Freeman, *Contesting Catholicity: Theology for Other Baptists* (Waco, TX: Baylor University Press, 2014); Barry Harvey, *Can These Bones Live? A Catholic Baptist Engagement with Ecclesiology, Hermeneutics, and Social Theory* (Grand Rapids, MI: Brazos, 2008); Paul S. Fiddes, Brian Haymes, and Richard Kidd, *Baptists and the Communion of Saints: A Theology of Covenanted Disciples* (Waco, TX: Baylor University Press, 2014); Brian Haymes, Ruth Gouldbourne, and Anthony R. Cross, *On Being the Church: Revisioning Baptist Identity* (Eugene, OR: Wipf and Stock, 2009). Of course, this article may also provide supporting material for this ongoing discussion.

[5] The vocabulary of "ecumenism" is not appropriate at this point, as it did not come into widespread use until later in the nineteenth century. "Catholic" and its cognates have a long history in the Baptist world. The seventeenth-century confessions use this language (see chapter twenty-six of the Second London Confession Faith of 1677 and articles twenty-nine and thirty of the *Orthodox Creed* of 1678), as does the "Bristol Tradition" that came to influence so much of the latter eighteenth-century and nineteenth-century Particular Baptists. Anthony R. Cross has done much to recover the history of the "Bristol Tradition." For more information, see Anthony R. Cross, "'To communicate simply you must understand profoundly': The Necessity of Theological Education for Deepening Ministerial Formation," *Journal of European Baptist Studies*, 19.1 (2019): 54–67; idem, "The Early Bristol Tradition as a Seedbed for Evangelical Reception among British Baptists, c. 1720–c. 1770," in *Pathways and Patterns in History: Essays on Baptists, Evangelicals, and the Modern World in Honour of David Bebbington*, ed. Anthony R. Cross, Peter J. Morden, and Ian M. Randall (Didcot, Oxfordshire: Baptist Historical Society, 2015), 50–77. For a use of the term closer to the time of Fuller himself, see the church covenant of the New Road Baptist Church, Oxford (Daniel Turner, *Charity the Bond of Perfection* [Oxford: J. Buckland, 1780], 22) and Robert Hall, Jr., *On Terms of Communion* (Philadelphia: Anthony Finley, 1816), 128.

[6] Michael A.G. Haykin, "'A Little Band of Brothers': Friendship in the Life of Andrew Fuller––An Essay on the Bicentennial of His Death," *Journal for Baptist Theology and Ministry* 12. 2 (2015): 10–13. In another place, Haykin comments on Fuller and his circle of friends: "This love of God for who he is, this emphasis on the revelation of his holiness in the cross, this evangelical catholicity that embraces all who are in Christ and this passion to see sinners saved were leading features not only of the spirituality of Pearce, but also of that of

General Baptist church in Market Harborough and later a missionary with the General Baptist Missionary Society, referred to Fuller as possessing "a mighty intellect, though not a very catholic heart."[7] The resolution to this uncertainty will be taken up later in the article.

Union of sentiments: The ground of union

It will be helpful to begin with Fuller's understanding of the key word "catholic." In his *Strictures on Sandemanianism*, Fuller describes the spirit of primitive Christianity as "*catholic* and *pacific*."[8] He elaborates on what it means to be "catholic" by juxtaposing it with "sectarian."[9] He writes, "True catholic zeal will nevertheless have the good of the universal church of Christ for its grand object, and will rejoice in the prosperity of every denomination of christians, *in so far* as they appear to have the mind of Christ."[10] To be "catholic," in Fuller's view, is to have a universal view of the work of Christ, and it is to rejoice when any denomination prospers, regardless of its connection to one's own theological and ecclesiastical commitments. It is to be broad-minded in affection; indeed, it is to keep in mind the whole of the church and feel the affection of kinship with it. Fuller places an important limit on his catholicity, however, by the introduction of the concept of "the mind of Christ."[11] While there is an element of

---

Fuller and Sutcliff" (*One Heart and One Soul: John Sutcliff of Olney, His Friends and His Times* [Darlington, Durham: Evangelical Press, 1994], 264).

[7] John Buckley, "Notes of Visits to the Churches, No. 4," *The General Baptist Magazine, Repository, and Missionary Observer* 1.3 (March 1854): 147.

[8] Andrew Fuller, *Strictures on Sandemanianism* (New York: Richard Scott, 1812), 212, emphasis original. For more information on Sandemanianism, see John Howard Smith, *The Perfect Rule of the Christian Religion: A History of Sandemanianism in the Eighteenth Century* (Albany, NY: State University of New York Press, 2008); Michael A.G. Haykin, "Sweet Sensibility: Andrew Fuller's Defense of Religious Affections," *Puritan Reformed Journal*, 7.2 (2015): 193–211; and Dyron Daughrity, "Glasite versus Haldanite: Scottish Divergence on the Question of Missions," *Restoration Quarterly* 53.2 (2011): 65–79.

[9] Fuller seems to have understood these terms in light of one another, as in another place he writes of "the disinterested testimony of a few people, who are united together, not by a sectarian, but a truly catholic spirit" (Andrew Fuller [A Dissenter], *A Vindication of Protestant Dissent* [London: Button and Son, 1803], 31). This work was attributed to "A Dissenter" when it was first published, but it was subsequently published in Fuller's *Complete Works*.

[10] Fuller, *Strictures on Sandemanianism*, 214, emphasis original. Fuller goes on to clarify what he does not mean by using the term "catholic," saying that "it is not our being of the religion of Rome, nor of any other which happens to be favoured by the state, that determines our zeal to be catholic" (Fuller, *Strictures on Sandemanianism*, 214). While it is unlikely that any of his readers would mistake Fuller for a Roman Catholic sympathiser, he apparently wanted to leave no room whatsoever for a mistake.

[11] He repeats this emphasis on the mind of Christ in a meditation on Ecclesiastes 1:15: "There are few things more spoken against in the present times, than *party zeal*; but there are few things more common. To unite with those whom we consider on mature examination as being nearest the mind of Christ, and having

broadness and even openness to Fuller's thought, the mind of Christ becomes a boundary-establishing element of his catholicity.

Fuller repeats the emphasis on the "mind of Christ" in other works, which help to flesh out his meaning. In his work defending strict communion, he indicates that 'the mind of Christ' refers to "the precepts and examples of the New Testament."[12] He summarises these precepts and examples, saying:

> If language have any determinate meaning, it is here plainly taught that mankind are not only sinners, but in a *lost* and perishing condition, without help or hope, but what arises from the free grace of God, through the atonement of his Son; that he died as our substitute; that we are forgiven and accepted only for the sake of what he hath done and suffered; that in his person and work all evangelical truth concentrates; that the doctrine of salvation for the chief of sinners through his death, was so familiar in the primitive times, as to become a kind of Christian proverb, or 'saying;' and that on our receiving and retaining this, depends our present standing and final salvation.[13]

This brief summary of evangelical doctrine is what Fuller considered to be the mind of Christ that served to bound his catholicity. That he would summarise it so is unsurprising in light of his Calvinistic Baptist convictions, but it is nevertheless worth establishing definitively that Fuller uses the phrase "the mind of Christ" as a kind of shorthand to encompass these propositions.[14] Indeed, he says as much when he comments that the early church "considered the doctrine of the person and work of Christ as a golden link, that would draw along with it the whole chain of evangelical truth."[15]

---

done so to act up to our principles,—is our duty" (Andrew Fuller, "Irremediable Evils" in *The Complete Works of the Rev. Andrew Fuller*, ed. by Joseph Belcher [Philadelphia: American Baptist Publication Society, 1845], 1:466–469, 467 [emphasis original]).

[12] Andrew Fuller, *The Admission of Unbaptized Persons to the Lord's Supper, Inconsistent with the New Testament* (London: H. Teape, 1815), 29.

[13] Andrew Fuller, *An Essay on Truth: Containing an Inquiry into Its Nature and Importance* (Boston, MA: Manning and Loring, 1806), 5.

[14] His friend John Ryland, Jr. outlines what he considered essential evangelical doctrine in much the same way (John Ryland, Jr., *The Practical Influence of Evangelical Religion* [London: J.G. Fuller, 1819], 6–14).

[15] Fuller, *Essay on Truth*, 6. In an essay on the deity of Christ, Fuller again makes Christ the central theme of any Christian union, saying, "And where these things are rejected, there is no longer any possibility of Christian union: for how can those, who consider Christ to be a mere man, join in the worship of such as are employed in calling upon his name, and ascribing blessing and honour, and glory and power, unto the Lamb for ever!" (Andrew Fuller, "Deity of Christ Essential to Our Calling on His Name and Trusting in Him for Salvation" in *Works*, 3:695–697).

Fuller's catholicity rests on mutual commitment to these doctrines, as he states that communion with other Christians arises out of "a union of sentiments in apostolical doctrines."[16] His understanding of catholicity is rooted in shared theological convictions. In a letter written to Samuel Palmer on the "bond of Christian union," Fuller makes the connection between a shared understanding of the truth and union explicit, saying, "Christian love appears to me to be, 'for the truth sake that dwelleth in us.' Every kind of union that has not truth for its bond, is of no value in the sight of God, and ought to be of none in ours."[17] Agreement as to the truth is the bond of union.[18]

The practice and limitations of catholicity
As mentioned above, Fuller often saw a catholic spirit in contrast to a sectarian, or party, spirit. He writes that, while a good person will no doubt unite "with that denomination of Christians whose sentiments he believes to be nearest the truth," such a person will not limit their affection to that denomination but will "love all who love Jesus Christ."[19] Fuller makes a distinction here, however, that reveals much about how he practised and limited his openness to others. There is *union* with those whose sentiments are closest to one's own, but there is only a *general love* for those who love Jesus Christ. While that may seem a pedantic distinction, it proves to be closest to Fuller's own practice, which showcases both his willingness to bridge the gap between himself and others who differ from him, as well as the boundaries of that willingness.

On the one hand, Fuller could readily overlook significant theological differences in others, affirm them, and even promote their work, so long as he discerned the mind of Christ being expressed in them. Three examples of this may be adduced. First, one may look to Fuller and the Arminians, of whom he was a vocal opponent, asserting in one place that they "can find but little use for the doctrinal part of Paul's Epistles," and in another categorising them together with Arians, Socinians, and traitors, whilst characterising them as heady,

---

[16] Andrew Fuller, "On Spiritual Declension and the Means of Revival" in *Works*, 3:630.

[17] Andrew Fuller, "Agreement in Sentiment the Bond of Christian Union" in *Works*, 3:490.

[18] Fuller appeals to the King James translation of Amos 3:3 (KJV): "Can two walk together except they be agreed?" (Andrew Fuller, "Agreement in Sentiment" in *Works*, 3:491). He says that this is the "force and design" of that passage, though modern translations reflect a different understanding of the Hebrew, signalling less an agreement as to sentiment and more an agreement as to walk together. For example, the New International Version has "Do two walk together unless they have agreed to do so?" The New Revised Standard Version translates it, "Do two walk together unless they have made an appointment?"

[19] Andrew Fuller, "Nature and Importance of Christian Love" in *Works*, 1:523. Once again, Fuller shows that truth may be apprehended but never comprehended.

high-minded, and lovers of their own selves.[20] However, he says that he "saw those whom I thought to be godly men, both among Arminians and High, or, as I now accounted them Hyper Calvinists."[21] That Fuller could speak of godly men among the Arminians in light of his words against them and their theology speaks to his willingness to "rejoice in the prosperity of every denomination of Christians," even if they differed significantly.[22]

Second, Fuller's catholicity is seen in his promotion of the work of the Edwardsean theologians from America, who were, by and large, those with whom Fuller would have refused to share the Lord's table.[23] Though Edwards was a paedobaptist and his followers tended to move in theological directions with which Edwards himself might have been uncomfortable, Fuller admired and did not hesitate to promote their works, sometimes in a very shrewd, calculating manner.[24] At one point in 1802, Fuller had in his possession something written by Jonathan Edwards, Jr., but he delayed in sending it to be published because "it w^d. be introducing American divinity in such a form as most English minds w^d. revolt at it. I w^d. rather preserve it as a lump of good materials that may be used in a different form to a good purpose."[25] Fuller's promotion of Edwards stemmed from his belief that Edwards had captured the essence of the mind of Christ in his work, regardless of Fuller's disagreement with him on other points.[26]

Third, Fuller had no problem preaching in the pulpits of those with whom

---

[20] Andrew Fuller, "Remarks on Two Sermons by W.W. Horne of Yarmouth," in *Works*, 3:583; Fuller, *Vindication of Protestant Dissent*, 21.

[21] Andrew Fuller, "Letter IV" in John Ryland, Jr., *Work of Faith, the Labour of Love, and the Patience of Hope, Illustrated; in the Life and Death of Andrew Fuller*, 2nd ed. (London: Button and Son, 1818), 28–29.

[22] Fuller, *Strictures on Sandemanianism*, 214.

[23] This would include the works of Jonathan Edwards, Sr., and also those of Jonathan Edwards, Jr., Samuel Hopkins, and Joseph Bellamy.

[24] See the series of essays which cover the stream of Edwardsean theology after Edwards in Oliver D. Crisp and Douglas A. Sweeney, eds., *After Jonathan Edwards: The Courses of the New England Theology* (New York: Oxford University Press, 2012).

[25] Andrew Fuller to John Sutcliff, January 11, 1802 (Angus Library and Archive, Regent's Park College, Oxford). In the letter, Fuller refers to "Dr Edwards" rather than "Jonathan Edwards, Jr.," but "Dr Edwards" was the name used to refer to the son and "President Edwards" was the name used to refer to the father.

[26] When he was criticised for his love for Edwards, Fuller responded with words that reveal the reason behind his affection: "We have some, who have been giving out of late, that 'If Sutcliff and some others had preached more of Christ, and less of Jonathan Edwards, they would have been more useful.' If those who talk thus, preached Christ half as much as Jonathan Edwards did, and were half as useful as he was, their usefulness would be double what it is. It is very singular that the Mission to the East should have originated with men of these principles" (John Ryland, Jr., *The Indwelling and Righteousness of Christ no Security against Corporeal Death, but the Source of Spiritual and Eternal Life* [London: Button and Son, 1815], 34).

he disagreed. He suffered no qualms about preaching in the pulpits of the Establishment, even admitting that, in so doing, he "materially served the mission" of the Church of England.[27] Fuller also preached in the pulpits of General Baptists, most notably that of Dan Taylor, the General Baptist against whom Fuller wrote repeatedly.[28] Indeed, when Fuller was given the option of preaching in Taylor's or another's pulpit, he commented, "I had much rather preach in Mr. T.'s pulpit, to convince the world that perfect cordiality subsists between him and myself."[29]

While Fuller could be broad-minded in some regards, his catholicity had decided limitations. Again, three examples will suffice to demonstrate this contention. First, his position against open communion has already been mentioned, but it is worth considering at this point that his strict-communionism meant that whatever ecclesiastical union Fuller sought with those with whom he differed ended with the issue of baptism.[30] While affirming of paedobaptists as fellow believers, he was at variance with John Ryland, Jr., who not only affirmed their faith but welcomed them to the Lord's table.[31] According to Fuller, while he could respect the principles of those who differed, if their sentiments on that subject were not united, then there could be no fellowship in the Lord's supper.[32] Indeed, his promotion of Edwardsean literature may well have been more ardent because of their geographical distance from Fuller himself: it would be unlikely that he would ever have to deal with an American Edwardsean at the Lord's table in Kettering.

---

[27] Fuller, "Agreement in Sentiment" in *Works*, 3:489.

[28] See Michael A.G. Haykin, "'The Honour of the Spirit's Work': Andrew Fuller, Dan Taylor, and an Eighteenth-Century Baptist Debate over Regeneration," *The Baptist Quarterly* 47.4 (2016): 152–161. It is not clear if Fuller ever returned the favour and allowed either a Church of England minister or Arminian to preach from his pulpit.

[29] Adam Taylor, ed., *Memoirs of the Rev. Dan Taylor* (London: Baynes and Son, 1820), 177. It should be noted that Fuller did not preach during the Sunday services for Taylor's church; rather, he preached for their Sunday School and Society for Visiting the Sick.

[30] See Fuller, *Admission of Unbaptized Persons*. See also Ian Hugh Clary, "'Throwing away the Guns': Andrew Fuller, William Ward, and the Communion Controversy in the Baptist Mission Society," *Foundations* 68 (2015): 84–101.

[31] John Ryland, Jr., *A Candid Statement of the Reasons which Induce the Baptists to Differ in Opinion and Practice from So Many of Their Christian Brethren* (London: W. Button, 1814), x–xi.

[32] In his work defending strict communion, he writes: "I am willing to allow that open communion *may* be practised from a conscientious persuasion of its being the mind of Christ; and they ought to allow the same of strict communion" (Fuller, *Admission of Unbaptized Persons*, 29). He is willing to allow that they are seeking to know the mind of Christ and that they are living in light of their understanding. Fuller shows his Baptist convictions here, for each must follow their understanding of the mind of Christ, being bound by their own conscience to do so, and Fuller is not willing to intrude upon the conscience of others.

A second limitation in Fuller's practice of catholicity is seen in the give and take of life as a pastor and denominational leader, for Fuller's relationships with other Christians were not always marked by peace and concord. This is seen clearly in the breakdown of his relationship with the church in Soham. Toward the end of his tenure as pastor of that church, Fuller writes to John Sutcliff regarding the tense situation with the church, "I continue far from happy, yet not so generally distressed as I was some weeks ago. I know not but I must remove at Michelmas yet can't tell how I shall get through it."[33] This breakdown between Fuller and his church is illustrative of the real-world limitations of catholicity imposed by human frailty.[34] Even the most catholic of souls may find their broadness of love challenged by the real world of actual human relationships, though Fuller may have faced greater challenges in that regard than others. His own close friends speak of his temperament as one that could veer towards the severe: "His natural temper might occasionally lead him to indulge too much severity, especially if it were provoked by the appearance of vanity or conceit [...] He was not a man, however, to be brow-beaten and overborne, when satisfied of the goodness of his cause; nor could he be easily imposed upon by any one."[35]

Third, while Fuller gave much of his life to the promotion of the work of missions with the Baptist Missionary Society (BMS), he felt no compulsion either to partner with other societies or to allow those with whom he differed theologically to partner too closely with the BMS. The relationship between the General Baptists and the BMS is illustrative of these limitations. In 1812, J.G. Pike, pastor of the Brook Street General Baptist Church, wrote to Fuller about the possibility of the General Baptists sending one of their own to the mission field through the BMS. Fuller responded to this proposal in the negative, citing the need for unanimity between partners. While he does not explicitly say so in his response to Pike, there can be little doubt that Fuller's ideas about a union of sentiments played a large part in his response. Fuller knew that the General Baptists and the Particular Baptists differed in significant ways

---

[33] Andrew Fuller to John Sutcliff, August 15, 1781, Isaac Mann Collection (National Library of Wales).

[34] Another example of brokenness in relationships between those who were united in sentiments is seen in Fuller's relationship with John Rippon, a fellow Particular Baptist. Fuller did not always have a high view of Rippon, of whom he writes to Sutcliff, "We are all offended with him and have reason to be so. He had a letter fm. Carey wch he kept back fm us, & yet wanted ours [...] We must desire both the missionaries not to write any thing confidential to Rippon" (Andrew Fuller to John Sutcliff, January 22, 1795 [Angus Library and Archive, Regent's Park College, Oxford])

[35] Ryland, *Work of Faith*, x. Fuller had been a wrestler in his youth and "seldom met with a sout man without making an ideal comparison of strength, and possessing some of his former feelings in reference to its exercise" (John Webster Morris, *Memoirs of the Life and Writings of the Rev. Andrew Fuller* [Boston, MA: Lincoln and Edmands, 1830], 306). He seems to have carried the mindset of a wrestler wherever he went.

with regard to theological sentiments, and, while they might have been able to look past those disagreements at the start, they would not have been able to ignore them forever.[36] Therefore, there could be no full partnership between the General and Particular Baptists with regard to missions.

Understanding the catholicity of Fuller
What emerges from Fuller is a complex picture of catholic thought and practice. On the one hand, he decries a party spirit, but on the other, he could defend partisanship as necessary and good. In a brief letter to the editor of the *Theological and Biblical Magazine*, Fuller writes:

> There appears to be a mistaken idea, too commonly prevailing in the religious world at present, respecting what is called *a party spirit*. Many professors, while they endeavour to promote the interests of religion in *general*, too often neglect to pay attention which is due to the interest and welfare of that class or denomination of Christians in *particular*, with which they are or have been connected.[37]

Fuller here promotes what he considers a necessary partisanship, as a Christian is meant to promote the interests of the denomination to which they are connected, which connection springs from their closer union of sentiments. While he goes on to speak against the idea of a "candour" that drives people to abandon "*consistency* and *integrity*" in the name of unity, there still exists some tension between this contention of the goodness of party and what he says elsewhere about the evil of a party spirit.[38] The question he leaves unanswered is, where is the line between a good partisanship and a lamentable party spirit?

In light of the evidence, the boundary line of catholicity seems to be in the area of active partnership and practical union. Indeed, for Fuller, while a catholic spirit would lead a person to rejoice in the successes of those who differ, it did not necessarily entail full partnership in the work of the gospel. Again, the

---

[36] Indeed, Fuller's word to Pike is, "Tho' there were no disputes on the subject wherein we differed at present, yet the measures they proposed might occasion them: and unanimity was of great importance" (quoted in G.P.R. Prosser, "The Formation of the General Baptist Missionary Society," *Baptist Quarterly* 22.1 [1967]: 25).

[37] Andrew Fuller, "Party Spirit" in *Works*, 3:797. Emphasis original.

[38] Fuller goes on to say, "It is not uncommon to see one of these '*candid*' Christian professors keep at a distance from his own denomination, or party, where that denomination stands most in need of his countenance and support; while he associates with another party, which is sanctioned by numbers and worldly influence. And when the inconsistency of his conduct is hinted at, he will excuse himself by saying, in the cant phrase of the day, 'That it is his wish to promote the interests of religion in general, *and not to serve a party*'" (Fuller, "Party Spirit" in *Works*, 3:797).

relationship between the General Baptists and the BMS is illustrative. When Pike made the suggestion of sending General Baptist missionaries with the BMS, he seems to have anticipated a negative answer from Fuller, for he also suggested that if the General Baptists could not send one of their own missionaries to Bengal, the Serampore missionaries themselves should choose a native believer to whom the General Baptists might send £14 a year as well as send and receive correspondence. To this Fuller assents. His catholicity would not allow him fully to partner with the General Baptists because of their difference in sentiments. However, it did allow him to receive their funds and allow them a lesser participatory role.

The issue for Fuller seems to be the extent of practical union and the conferring of authority to the other. Because of his understanding of catholicity resting on a union of sentiments, Fuller is hesitant to extend the fullness of fellowship, partnership, and authority to those with whom he believed did not fully share (or, at least, significantly share) his theological commitments. If Fuller himself maintains the authority, and the other with whom he does not share sentiments is under that authority, he is more willing to "partner" with them. In other words, without a union of sentiments, Fuller is largely unwilling to treat the other as an equal partner. Union of sentiments, for Fuller, meant equality of partnership and authority.

Fuller's catholicity, then, is two-tiered. On the one hand, he is willing to embrace all who love the Lord Jesus in sincerity, and he warns against the insidious nature of a party spirit. On the other hand, he reserves co-labouring for those of his theological side, or at least for those with whom he is most in agreement.

Assessing Fuller's catholicity

This outline of Fuller's catholicity suggests two questions that must be answered. First, there is the question of Fuller's relation to his own historical context: how does Fuller fit into his own time? The catholicity of John Ryland, Jr may function as a contrast and counterpoint to Fuller. Ryland's openness to those outside of his tradition, sometimes well outside, has been noted by both his contemporaries as well as recent scholars.[39] His catholicity, however, was not like that of Fuller. Whereas Fuller roots his openness in a union of sentiments, Ryland finds his connection with other believers at the level of experience. He

---

[39] Robert Hall, Jr., "A Sermon Occasioned by the Death of the Rev. John Ryland, D.D. Preached at the Baptist Meeting, Broadmead, Bristol, June 5, 1825," in *The Works of the Rev. Robert Hall, A.M.*, ed. Olinthus Gregory (New York: Harper, 1832), 1:217; Michael A.G. Haykin, "'The Sum of All Good': John Ryland, Jr. and the Doctrine of the Holy Spirit," *Churchman* 103 (1989): 343–348; Christopher W. Crocker, "The Life and Legacy of John Ryland, Jr. (1753–1825), a Man of Considerable Usefulness: An Historical Biography" (PhD diss., University of Bristol, 2018), 331–360; Lon Graham, "'All Who Love Our Blessed Redeemer': The Catholicity of John Ryland, Jr." (PhD diss., Vrije Universiteit Amsterdam, 2021).

writes that "so far as we can obtain evidence of godly sincerity, and a cordial union with Christ, we ought to take pleasure in the communion of faith, by the acknowledging of every good thing which is in our brethren toward Christ Jesus."[40] Whereas Ryland sought a catholicity in the shared experience of Christ and the Spirit, Fuller seeks shared theological convictions.[41] In the end, this leaves Fuller with considerably less openness to those who differ than Ryland, who not only preached in the pulpits of General Baptists, Methodists, Presbyterians, and the Establishment but also supported Wesleyan missionary societies and recommended Arminians to the mission field.

Much the same can be said when Fuller is compared with another contemporary, John Wesley. In his sermon on a "Catholic Spirit," Wesley speaks to the "peculiar love which we owe to those that love God."[42] While he is keen to maintain a special connection to a local congregation, he nevertheless exhorts his hearers to love others who have a "heart right with God" and who show that right-heartedness both in orthodoxy and orthopraxy.[43] This love, according to Wesley, entails more than well-wishing and a general positivity toward the other; in Wesley's words, it should not be "in word only, but in deed and in truth."[44] He then says that the person of a catholic spirit will join with others in the work of God, and "go on hand in hand."[45]

While these two contemporaries of Fuller may be said to be more liberal in their catholicity, it should also be recognised that Fuller is not out of line with his Particular Baptist forebears. Indeed, his practice is much closer to the majority of them than is Ryland's. Michael Haykin has made the argument that the Particular Baptist churches were seen as "enclosed gardens," separated from

---

[40] John Ryland, Jr., "The Communion of Saints," *Pastoral Memorials* (London: B.J. Holdsworth, 1828), 2:280. In a letter to Stephen West, Ryland makes the same point in much the same language: "I trust I do believe that all who are really sanctified have one common interest, and are, indeed, living members of one common body, of which our blessed Emmanuel is really the head, and are really animated by one Spirit" (Ryland, "Letter to Stephen West" [March 31, 1814], *Bibliotheca Sacra* 30.117 (January 1873), 181.

[41] For more on this, see Graham, "All Who Love Our Blessed Redeemer," 157–84.

[42] John Wesley, "Catholic Spirit" in *The Works of the Rev. John Wesley* (New York: Harper, 1826), 5:410.

[43] Wesley, "Catholic Spirit" in *Works*, 5:414-415. Wesley says that a heart that is right with God will believe such things as God's being, perfections, eternity, immensity, wisdom, power, justice, mercy, and truth. Such a person will also hold to the divinity of Jesus, justification by faith, and the crucifixion. He goes on to speak of possessing a faith that is "filled with the energy of love" and which is "employed in doing 'not thy own will, but the will of him that sent thee." He includes a person's labour, business, and conversation in this description of a right heart.

[44] Wesley, "Catholic Spirit" in *Works*, 5:417.

[45] Wesley, "Catholic Spirit" in *Works*, 5:417. He summarises his understanding, saying, "a man of a catholic spirit is one who [...] gives his hand to all whose hearts are right with his heart" (Wesley, "Catholic Spirit" in *Works*, 5:419).

the world.[46] With regard to the majority of such churches and their practice, Haykin is surely correct. In the seventeenth century, Benjamin Keach wrote the following:

> Some part of a wilderness hath been turned into a garden or fruitful vineyard: so God hath out of the people of this world, taken his churches and walled them about, that none of the evil beasts can hurt them: all mankind naturally were alike dry and barren, as a wilderness, and brought forth no good fruit. But God hath separated some of this barren ground, to make lovely gardens for himself to walk and delight in.[47]

In the eighteenth century, John Gill wrote, "the church is like an "enclosed" garden; for distinction, being separated by the grace of God, in election, redemption, effectual calling and for protection, being encompassed with the power of God, as a wall about it; and for secrecy, being so closely surrounded, that it is not to be seen nor known by the world."[48] Fuller's practice, if not his theological reasoning, reflects this enclosed nature.[49]

While Fuller would not have been considered out of step with those who came before him, his views would find decreasing acceptance in the future of Particular Baptist life. One year after Fuller's death, Robert Hall, Jr. argued for open communion on the basis of catholic principles, stating:

> But since the Holy Ghost identifies that body with the church, explaining the one by the other, ("for his body's sake, which is the church,") it seems impossible to deny that they are fully entitled to be considered in the catholic sense of the term, as members of the Christian church. And as the universal church is nothing more than the colective [sic] body of the faithful, and differs only from a particular assembly of Christians, as

---

[46] Michael A.G. Haykin, "'A Garden Inclosed': Worship and Revival among the English Particular Baptists of the Eighteenth Century," Unpublished Lecture, February 28, 2008, The Southern Baptist Theological Seminary, Louisville Kentucky (https://equip.sbts.edu/event/lectures/icw/contemporary-baptist-worship-in-the-18th-century-1680s-1830s; accessed on January 30, 2021), 2–4.

[47] Benjamin Keach, *Gospel Mysteries Unveiled: or, an Exposition of All the Parables, and Many Express Similitudes, Spoken by Our Lord and Savior Jesus Christ* (Repr. London: E. Justins, 1815), 2:232.

[48] John Gill, *An Exposition of the Old Testament* (Repr. London: Mathews and Leigh, 1810), 4:662; also see Haykin, *One Heart and One Soul*, 20.

[49] Fuller, however, is more liberal in his openness than Gill. While Fuller was willing to preach in the pulpits of the Establishment, Gill wrote that the Church of England was "very corrupt, and not agreeable to the word of God" (John Gill, *The Dissenter's Reasons for Separating from the Church of England* [London, 1760], 3), adding that it "cannot be a true church of Christ" (Gill, *The Dissenter's Reasons for Separating from the Church of England*, 5).

the whole from a part, it is equally impossible to deny that a Pædobaptist society is, in the more limited import of the word, a true church.[50]

Hall's argument rests on understanding "catholic" as referring to the whole, universal church, and such catholicity, argues Hall, entails a much more robust acceptance of differences than that found in Fuller. If a paedobaptist is a member of the universal church, so goes Hall's reasoning, then societies of them must also be considered as expressions of the true church. Therefore, they ought to be treated as such. The belief in the catholic or universal church leads to an openness to, acceptance of, fellowship and partnership with all who are a part of that church. Subsequent history shows that the catholicity of Ryland and Hall would shape the denomination rather than that of Fuller.[51]

The second question concerns the concept of catholicity itself, as applied to Fuller's thinking and practice. This article earlier referred to the comment of Buckley that Fuller did not possess "a very catholic heart."[52] Is Buckley correct? Like Fuller's thoughts on this issue, the answer is not straightforward. If Fuller is allowed to define his own terms, and catholicity is understood as seeking "the good of the universal church of Christ" and "rejoic[ing] in the prosperity of every denomination of Christians," then there is a sense in which it is proper to call Fuller's thought and practice "catholic," as he did do those things.[53] Thus, considered on his own terms, it is fair to deem Fuller to have possessed a kind of catholicity.

However, it is worth considering whether Fuller's practice was consistent with his own terms. As noted above, he sets the "mind of Christ" as an important limitation of his catholicity.[54] According to his own definition of the mind of Christ, Arminians and paedobaptists need not be excluded, yet Arminians did not enjoy full partnership with Fuller, and he did not welcome paedobaptists to the Lord's table. He was, thus, inconsistent within his own definition.

This then raises a final question: was Fuller's practice simply denominationalism without party spirit, rather than a version of catholicity?[55] If "denominationalism" refers to a commitment to one's own denomination over against

---

[50] Hall, *Terms of Communion*, 105.

[51] Interestingly, Raymond Brown has argued that it was Fuller's modification of Calvinism that allowed this merger to occur (Raymond Brown, *The English Baptists of the Eighteenth Century* [London: Baptist Historical Society, 1986], 112).

[52] Buckley, "Notes of Visits to the Churches, No. 4," 147.

[53] Buckley, "Notes of Visits to the Churches, No. 4," 147.

[54] Buckley, "Notes of Visits to the Churches, No. 4," 147.

[55] With thanks to an anonymous reviewer for this phrase.

others, then Fuller's restrictions are more than mere denominationalism. Ryland was committed to the same denomination as Fuller, and sought to advance its interests as well, but that did not bar him from extending his partnerships to those outside of it.[56] Fuller's limitations were less about denomination and more about theological commitments, as he was concerned more about doctrinal sentiments than denomination. Indeed, in one letter, Fuller explicitly denies what might be called "denominationalism." Writing to the pastor of the Baptist church in New York, John Williams, Fuller thanks Williams for the kindness that the Americans had shown to unnamed BMS missionaries on their way to Bengal.[57] Fuller explained to Williams the importance that he attached to this particular mission, saying"

> We consider the mission to Bengal as the most favourable symptom attending our denomination. It confirms what has been for some time with me an important principle, that where any denomination, congregation, (or individual) seeks only *its own*, it will be disappointed: but where it seeks the kingdom of God and his righteousness, its own prosperity will be among the things that will be added unto it.[58]

His interest was more about doctrinal purity than denominational protectionism.

Conclusion

Fuller's catholicity was nuanced. It possessed limitations that kept it from being expressed in significant ways. While he could support the efforts of those with whom he differed, he did so from a distance, never entering into a full partnership with them, nor embracing them fully as a fellow believer at the table of the Lord. His concept of a union of sentiments demonstrates that he could not unite with those with whom he truly differed, thus showing that his

---

[56] To make matters more complex, according to John Ryland, Jr., the "Particular Baptist" denomination contained some Arminian churches among them (John Ryland, Jr. to Unknown Recipient, February 26, 1806 [Yale University Library]). Ryland notes that there were ten or twelve such churches that leaned toward Arminianism.

[57] Based on the date of the letter, these missionaries were most likely Richard Mardon, John Biss, William Moore, and Joshua Rowe, along with their wives (Francis Augustus Cox, *History of the Baptist Missionary Society, from 1792 to 1842* [London: T. Ward, 1842], 1:137).

[58] Andrew Fuller to John Williams, August 1, 1804 (American Baptist Historical Society Archive). This letter has been published several times: Andrew Fuller, "Interesting Intelligence from India," *The Massachusetts Baptist Missionary Magazine* 1.4 (May 1805): 97–98; Leighton Williams, and Mornay Williams, ed., *Serampore Letters: Being the Unpublished Correspondence of William Carey and Others with John Williams* (New York: Fleming H. Revell, 1892); Michael A.G. Haykin, *The Armies of the Lamb: The Spirituality of Andrew Fuller* (Dundas, ON: Joshua Press, 2001), 193–195.

attitude was shaped less by a robust catholicity and more by a tolerance based on an unwillingness to violate another's conscience.[59] While conscience-based tolerance is important, it is, arguably, not necessarily catholic.

He was open in his love for all those who called on the name of Christ and rejoiced in their prosperity, but he was careful not to cast his net too wide, as he also describes approach to union with other Christians in contrast to what he has heard others promote, saying:

> I have heard a great deal of *union without sentiment*; but I can neither feel nor perceive any such thing, either in myself or others. All the union that I can feel or perceive, arises from *a similarity of views and pursuits*. No two persons may think exactly alike; but so far as they are unlike, so far there is a want of union.[60]

This speaks clearly to the distinctions to be found in Fuller's thought: unity is on a sliding scale of agreement as to the mind of Christ, and the greater the unity, the greater the equality in partnership enjoyed. For Fuller, if there was sufficient agreement between believers, then full (or a fuller) fellowship and partnership could be extended and fostered. However, in the absence of such agreement, Fuller, while not willing to treat other believers with indifference, would not extend the fullness of fellowship to them.

---

[59] The literature on "tolerance" is voluminous. Just a selection of more recent works reveals a wide array of approaches to its history and theory: Teresa M. Bijan, *Mere Civility: Disagreement and the Limits of Toleration* (Cambridge, MA: Harvard University Press, 2017); John Coffey, *Persecution and Toleration in Protestant England, 1558-1689* (London: Routledge, 2000); Jakob De Roover and S.N. Balagangadhara, "John Locke, Christian Liberty, and the Predicament of Liberal Toleration," *Political Theory* 36.4 (2008): 523-549; Ole Peter Grell, and Roy Porter, *Toleration in Enlightenment Europe* (Cambridge: Cambridge University Press, 2000); Marjoka van Doorn, "The Nature of Tolerance and the Social Circumstances in Which It Emerges," *Current Sociology Review* 62. 6 (2014): 905-927; Alexandra Walsham, *Charitable Hatred: Tolerance and Intolerance in England, 1500-1700* (Manchester: Manchester University Press, 2006); Robert Louis Wilken, *Liberty in the Things of God: The Christian Origins of Religious Freedom* (New Haven, CT: Yale University Press, 2019); Perez Zagorin, *How the Idea of Religious Toleration Came to the West* (Princeton, NJ: Princeton University Press, 2005). Future research into the influence of the Enlightenment on Fuller's thinking would no doubt prove fruitful.

[60] Fuller, "Agreement in Sentiment" in *Works*, 3:491.

Texts & documents

"Writing to George Whitefield: A letter from Anne Dutton on sinless perfection"

Edited and introduced by Michael A.G. Haykin

Michael A.G. Haykin is the Chair and professor of church history at The Southern Baptist Theological Seminary.

George Whitefield was a consummate "networker." By the warmth of his personality and his penchant for friendship, he was able to not only traverse the Atlantic to yoke together like-minded evangelicals but also cross the great divide of denominations. In Great Britain and throughout the American colonies, for example, he built relationships with Baptists, who viewed Anglicanism with a significant degree of distrust and dislike, but who loved Whitefield, the "Grand Itinerant." Among his English Baptist friends was Anne Dutton (1692–1765), who has been well described as "perhaps the most theologically capable and influential Baptist woman of her day" and who regularly corresponded with Whitefield between 1740 and 1744.[1]

---

[1] Karen O'Dell Bullock, "Dutton [née Williams], Anne," *Oxford Dictionary of National Biography*, Oxford University Press, 2004; online ed., January 2009, http://www.oxforddnb.com.libaccess.lib.mcmaster.ca/view/article/71063 (accessed on July 9, 2014). Dutton wrote a significant number of works. Most of them have survived in only a few copies. Thankfully, the most important of her works are currently available in an edition being published by Mercer University Press: JoAnn Ford Watson, *Selected Spiritual Writings of Anne Dutton: Eighteenth-Century, British-Baptist, Woman Theologian* (2003–2015), 7 vols. For an excellent study of her life, piety, and influence, see also Michael D. Sciretti, Jr., "'Feed My Lambs': The Spiritual Direction

One of the key theological issues that occupied Whitefield during this very time was the matter of Christian perfection. The Wesley brothers, John and Charles, were maintaining that God bestowed a second blessing, as it were, which consisted of being free from sin in thought, word, and deed. While neither of the brothers ever claimed to have received this blessing personally, and Charles later in the 1760s openly questioned the biblical legitimacy of his brother's position on this matter, in the early 1740s both Methodist leaders argued that as this doctrinal distinctive was preached, God honored the preaching and gave the gift.

Whitefield seems to have communicated his disagreement with this teaching to Dutton, who responded with this tightly packed and biblically reasoned letter on why sinless perfection was not at all correct theologically. Here we see why Whitefield once noted that Dutton's letters were weighty and how Dutton helped the great evangelist to think through this issue biblically and stand firm in his convictions.[2] The original of this letter is undated, but it would have been written most probably in 1740 before Whitefield wrote his famous reply to John Wesley's *Free Grace* on Christmas Eve of that year.[3]

Text

Right glad am I, that our dear Lord has brought you to Bristol, enables you so frequently, and successfully to labor in his gospel, and manifests his presence with you there. Now sir, you are in the heat of battle. But since Christ is with you, fear not. O poor Bristol! How have many there been deluded by sin and Satan, in such a manner, as to think they have no sin. For indeed sir, I can look upon it to be no other than a delusion of the enemy of souls, and a deceit of the heart, for any to think, that there is such a thing attainable in this life, as an entire, sinless perfection; and much more so, for any to think, that they

---

Ministry of Calvinistic British Baptist Anne Dutton During the Early Years of the Evangelical Revival" (PhD diss., Baylor University, 2009). See the detailed examination of their extant correspondence by Sciretti, "Feed My Lambs," 241–273.

[2] For JoAnn Ford Watson's edition of the letter, see *Selected Spiritual Writings of Anne Dutton*, 1:1–4. In the edit that follows, I have followed *A Letter from Mrs. Anne Dutton to The Reverend Mr. G. Whitefield* (Philadelphia, PA: William Bradford, n.d.). The text has been modernized when it comes to capitalization, spelling, and the use of italics and punctuation. I have also added quotation marks for biblical quotes and updated the method of citing biblical texts.

[3] George Whitefield, *A Letter from the Reverend Mr. George Whitefield, to the Reverend Mr. John Wesley, in Answer to his Sermon, entituled Free Grace* (Boston, MA: S. Kneeland and T. Green, J. Edwards and S. Eliot, 1740). For the text of Wesley to which this, and Anne Dutton's letter, are responses, see John Wesley, *Free Grace: A Sermon preach'd at Bristol* (Bristol: S. and F. Farley, 1739). Wesley's sermon was reprinted the following year in London by W. Strahan.

themselves have attained it. Strange it is, that any should think, or affirm, that they have not sinned in thought, word or deed for months! And stranger still, and what I never before heard of, that any should imagine that the being of sin is taken out of their nature! But what blindness and hardness, will not Satan and sin cast upon our souls, if permitted! Surely this error is now come to its height, and the time come that the enemy shall proceed no further. Surely Satan shall fall like lightning from heaven. Our Lord suffers the enemy to go to the end of his chain, to drive on his designs so far till he thinks he has got souls fast enough in his snare; and then he delights to confound him, and let the captives go free! Verily our dear Lord, will redeem the souls of his children from deceit and violence, their lives being precious in his sight. Do your utmost, my dear brother, to disentangle the ensnared in Bristol. For the delusion which prevails, will have most pernicious consequences. And that it is a delusion, the Word of God most clearly manifests.

For "if we say that we have no sin," (says the Apostle John) "we deceive ourselves, and the truth is not in us," 1 John 1:8. And says the Holy Ghost by Solomon, "there is not a just man upon the earth that doeth good, and sinneth not," Eccles 7:20. The great work of the Grace of God, which bringeth salvation to the saved ones is teaching them, that denying "ungodliness and worldly lusts, they should live soberly, righteously, and godly in this present world," Titus 2:11-12. The word *teaching*, being in the present tense, denotes the constant work of divine grace upon the subjects thereof, while they are in this world. The word *denying*, denotes the constant duty, and business of Christians, so long as they are in this present world. And the teaching of grace to deny ungodliness, and the denying of the same, both being of equal duration with the stay of Christians in this present world: do necessarily imply, the being, and solicitations of ungodliness, and worldly lusts in their souls, even so long as they are in the body, or in this present world. To deny a person or thing supposes the being and solicitations of that person or thing. So to deny ungodliness and worldly lusts supposes the being and solicitations thereof. And as a Christian's work, his constant work, lies in a continual denying of ungodliness, and worldly lusts; it must undeniably suppose the being, and solicitations of sin, so long as they are in this world. Thus, 2 Cor 7:1 "having these promises (dearly beloved) let us cleanse ourselves from all filthiness of the flesh and spirit", perfecting holiness in the fear of God: doth necessarily suppose our present impurity and imperfection, both in the soul and body, while in this life.

So also 1 John 3:3, "And every man that hath this hope in him, purifieth himself, even as he is pure," doth necessarily imply his present impurity while he is in this world, or until he enjoys the hoped for blessing, of seeing Christ as he is, else there would be no room to say of him, that he purifies himself. So likewise, our imperfection in holiness, which arises from the being and working of sin in our corrupt nature, is necessarily implied, ver. 2, where the Apostle says, "When he shall appear, we shall be like him; for we shall see him as he is." He doth not say we are like him; (no not us Apostles) but we shall be like him. And [he] gives the great cause of this great effect: for we shall see him as he is. Sight of Christ is the cause of likeness to him. Sight of Christ partial in this life produceth partial likeness. Sight of Christ total in the life to come will produce total likeness to him. First in our souls, during a separate state, and then in our whole persons after the resurrection of the just. Then, and not till then, shall we be perfectly like Christ, in holiness and glory. Holiness, which is the glory of the soul, is the effect of us beholding the glory of the Lord, as 2 Cor 3:18. But we all with open face, beholding "as in a glass the Glory of the Lord, are changed in the same image, from glory to glory, as by the Spirit of the Lord." Whence we may likewise note, that the change of the soul into the image of God, is imperfect, with respect to degrees, and a progressive work while in this life: it is from glory to glory. The New Testament saints, if compared with the Old, have an open-faced view of the glory of God in Christ; and a more glorious change into his image. But if compared with that vision of God which we shall have in glory, we see but darkly. And an inspired Apostle says, "Now I know in part, then (when that which is perfect is come, and that which is in part done away) shall I know, even as also I am known," 1 Cor 13:12. "Thou canst not see my face," says God to Moses, "for there shall no man" (let him be ever such a favourite) "see me and live," Exod 33:20.

Therefore no man can be perfect in holiness in this life. And in a word, a sinless perfection in this life thwarts the whole design of the Gospel with respect to the saints in the present state. For as soon as the Apostles had laid down the great doctrines of grace, the use they make thereof, to those interested in them, is holiness. From privilege, they press to duty; from grace to holiness, both in the mortification of sin and increase of grace, inward and outward, as is manifest in all their Epistles. So that I don't see, but if we admit of sinless perfection here; we may even throw[4] away our Bibles, certainly, if any persons had attained it, they would have no more need of ordinances. Nor can I see reason why such persons should be any longer out of heaven, when thus fully prepared for it.

That you may still increase with all the increases of God; both personally, and ministerially: And that all errors may fall before the rising glory of Truth is the hearty desire of,

Dear Sir, yours for ever in our Sweet Lord Jesus.

---

[4] At this point Dutton has "through," a misspelling for "throw."

The Journal of Andrew Fuller Studies
4 | February 2022

"You will scarcely need another intimate friend": A letter of James Hinton to his daughter, Ann, on her marriage[1]

Edited and introduced by Chance Faulkner

Chance Faulkner serves as a Junior Fellow of the Andrew Fuller Center for Baptist Studies and is a MTh candidate at Union School of Theology in Wales.

Introduction

The following letter is from James Hinton (1761–1823) to his daughter, Ann (née Hinton) Bartlett (1795–1866), on her marriage.[2] The letter is filled with fatherly affection and advice gained only from his own experience of a prosperous marriage.[3] He reminds her that though life will have "clouds and sorrows," these are only so that "heaven may not be forgotten." Though painful

---

[1] This letter is extracted from John Howard Hinton, *A Biographical Portraiture of the late Rev. James Hinton, M.A.* (Oxford: Bartlett and Hinton; London: B.J. Holdsworth, 1824), 67–71. Capitalization has been modernized.

[2] Ann married Thomas Bartlett, a co-witness along with Ann at the wedding of her brother, James Hinton Jr. (1793–1862), to Susannah Collingwood on May 15, 1821. When Ann was fourteen, she wrote a letter to her cousin Ann Taylor which is a fascinating look into her life in Oxford, particularly her education under James Hinton. See Ann Hinton, Letter to Ann Taylor, March 28, 1809, in Doris Mary Armitage, *The Taylors of* Ongar (Cambridge: W. Heffer & Sons, 1939), 19–21 note.

[3] Hinton had married Ann Taylor on April 23, 1790. Speaking of the wonders of marriage, Hinton tells Joseph Kinghorn (1766–1832) of Norwich, "Marriage absolutely is this world's paradise, with peace & purity." (James Hinton to Joseph Kinghorn, April 30, 1795, D/KIN 2/1795 no. 837 [Angus Library and Archives, Regent's Park College, Oxford University], 3).

and real, the trials of life are a means of taking our eyes off earthly things and pointing us to the glorious hopes of heaven. In addition, these sorrows provide the opportunity to recognize and acknowledge the bounty of blessings graciously given by the Lord.

Hinton also provides insight into potential future conflicts in marriage and encourages Ann to rely solely on God's sufficient grace so that the Accuser not have an opportunity to plant bitterness in her heart. He warns her against pride, which he argues can only be cured by studying the person of the Lord Jesus Christ who is lowly and meek in heart. He also offers advice on money, budgeting, hospitality, and the necessity of being generous, especially toward her husband. And since family relations can be a source of conflict, Hinton also urges her to speak well of her husband's relatives, yet without flattery. As a homemaker and helpmate to her future husband, Hinton emphasizes the importance of finding the balance between the domestic duties of the home while seeking to serve the cause of Christ publicly. He concludes the letter by advising Ann on the choice of her friends and to especially make her husband her most intimate friend.

Although this letter was written in the late 1810s, definitely before 1821, it still provides much wise counsel for twenty-first-century marriages. Though a different time, a different society, a different context, the difficulties of human relationships and the sinfulness of the human heart are the same. The letter provides another reason why eighteenth-century evangelicals are fit spiritual mentors—they continue to guide, instruct and counsel even long after they have entered their glorious rest.

Text
God grant, my dear child, that your days may run prosperously along, till all the felicities you have seen and shared in the society of your parents, shall have been enjoyed, and sanctified—improved to the highest and noblest purpose, of character matured for a dwelling in the skies. And why may I not be permitted to hope for you, my child, those smiles which all-gracious heaven has vouchsafed to your parents?[4] You are entering on this important connection, as they did, with a heart consecrated to God, their God and your God. His counsel you have chosen for your guide, his favour for your portion, his promise for the stay of your soul, his glory as the great end of your existence, his eternal smiles as the consummation of all your hopes; rely then on his word, "My presence shall go with thee, and I will surely do thee good."[5]

Do I judge your heart rightly when I fancy I hear you say, "But who can pass

---

[4] Sarah Hinton (1796–1813), their only other daughter, who died at the age of 17.

[5] Exodus 33:14.

through life without meeting with clouds and sorrows which oft[en] obscure the loveliest morning, without witnessing the blights which cut off the fairest hopes of spring? Why this frequent sounding knell? Why these children without a parent? Why these mourners that walk about the streets? Why all these dangers in the path to heaven?" … It is that heaven may not be forgotten. It is that far worse dangers than these may be removed; the danger of fixing on earth our highest love, of fancying this world our home, of neglecting to cherish communion with him whose friendship must be to us higher than the highest earthly joys. It is that amidst the solemn gloom of deep affliction, we may listen to the voice which saith, "The time is short; rejoice as though ye rejoiced not, weep as though ye wept not."[6] Let those who have dear connections retire and meditate as though they had none; let them not forget their first love,[7] nor fail to make every other subordinate to it, lest God see it and be offended and say, "Let them alone, they are turned away from me." And then, my child, O what is earth with all it joys? What years of woe will a backsliding heart create! O my daughter,

> Lean not on earth; 'twill pierce thee to the heart.
> A broken reed at best, but oft a spear![8]

Yet thankfully acknowledge the bounty of him who bestows your blessings. … Having committed your mortal and immortal interests to the care of the blessed God, whose promises will not deceive you, repeat this surrender every day; and then, without anticipating evil enjoy the blessings he bestows, only with the holy caution of recollecting that they are neither immutable nor immortal, but sent to lead to those that are so.

Circumstances vary, but the general principle of obedience will adapt itself to a thousand variations, and to this you will resort, and to its Author. You will study that every wish may be anticipated; yet, after all, man is not perfect, nor is more lovely woman entirely so. It is possible that your companion, harassed in business, disappointed and crossed by the concerns of the world, may (some seven years hence) come home without his usual smile upon his brow, or the accents of love upon his tongue; but do not listen to the suggestion that his love has grown cold. Such a thought, I trust, will never enter your breast; or, if an evil spirit suggest it, the generosity of your own mind will instantly spurn the accuser, while you hasten to sooth the spirit that is wounded, and to pour in the

---

[6] 1 Corinthians 7:30.

[7] Revelation 2:4.

[8] Edward Young, *The Complaint: Or, Night-thoughts: On Life, Death, and Immortality* ([London?], 1755), 51.

balm that will soon restore its wonted tone of tenderness and love. It is possible, too, that my child herself may in some unfortunate moment kindle at a spark, when it falls on a heart conscious, not only of integrity, but of tenderness, and wounded to the quick by a word, though uttered without a design to grieve. Trust not to nature, my love, where nothing but grace is sufficient. For want of this caution, I have seen many a temper, apparently calm and sweet, become turbulent or bitter; but this is never the case with one who studies closely the fair copy of his character who said, "Learn of me, for I am meek and lowly of heart."[9] If we are lowly we shall always be meek. It is hard to feel a consciousness of amiable and generous designs, without thinking too highly of ourselves on that account; and, though I wish you all true excellence of character, I must caution you against what is called pride of character, and is often justified under that name, when it ought to be condemned.

Will you allow me to suggest to you one word on temporals? You will, I trust, bend your mind from the first to all such economy as is consistent with real and well regulated generosity. You will inform yourself accurately of the amount of supplies; reckon these weekly, and then, reserving a portion for extraordinary occasions and times of affliction, firmly resolve that the remainder shall not be exceeded in your ordinary expense. The consolation of your own mind, the peace of your husband's mind, the prosperity of your concerns, and I will add, the glory of God, are all much more implicated in following this advice than it is usual for even good people to apprehend.

You will doubtless pay great attention to the relatives, particularly the sisters, of your husband, and treat them in every respect as your own. From the moment you are married you must scarcely suppose that they have any faults, and to their actual imperfections you must be blind, and deaf, and dumb; you must be all attention to their virtues, and uniformly speak of them with pleasure, though not with adulation.[10] Your husband will, in return, take very kind notice of your relations, and not a word that can be construed into a slight will, I trust, be heard on either side; this will greatly endear you to each other.

… Your acquaintance will be, as they have been, very select; you have learned that there are but few to whom you may commit all your heart. When married, your husband will, of course, possess your most entire confidence, and, besides your dear mother, you will scarcely need another intimate friend—of your domestic concerns it will be better not to speak to any besides; your conversation with your other female friends will be very kind, but very general. Female curiosity is very strong, particularly respecting a family so recently settled; and an open countenance and a moderately close heart, will greatly befriend your

---

[9] Matthew 11:29.

[10] Excessive admiration or flattery.

peace. A tattling spirit, if it beg around your door or watch your lips, should be starved for want of food, and it will cease to beset you. … I would recommend that, when you pay a visit, or receive one, the company should separate at an early hour, in order that the season of devotion may not be lost. … You will not, I trust, cease to be a friend to the poor whenever you can find opportunity; and you will not only relieve their temporal wants with such means as God may afford you, but speak to them on behalf of their best interests. Your husband will have his hands closely engaged; you may therefore suggest liberal things so that both you and he may avoid the extremes you have often observed—on the one hand, of so serving the public as to neglect domestic duties; on the other, of so attending to domestic concerns as to do nothing for the cause of Christ and the spread of religion.

The Journal of Andrew Fuller Studies
4 | February 2022

"Eminent piety, and ministerial ability": James Hinton to his son on pastoral ministry

Edited and introduced by Chance Faulkner

Chance Faulkner serves as a Junior Fellow of the Andrew Fuller Center for Baptist Studies and is an MTh candidate at Union School of Theology in Wales.

Introduction

The following letter was written by James Hinton (1761–1823) of Oxford around 1816 to his son while he was studying at the University at Edinburgh.[1] It was either written to his first-born and biographer, John Howard Hinton (1791–1873) or his third-born James Hinton Jr. (1793–1862), both of whom studied at Edinburgh and went into pastoral ministry.[2] In the letter, Hinton's

---

[1] This letter is extracted from John Howard Hinton, *A Biographical Portraiture of the late Rev. James Hinton, M.A.* (Oxford: Bartlett and Hinton; London: B.J. Holdsworth, 1824), 62–64. Capitalization and spelling have been modernized.

[2] John Howard Hinton ministered at Haverfordwest, Hosier Street Chapel, in Reading, and Devonshire Square Chapel in London, and was the first secretary of the Baptist Union. For more on John Howard Hinton see Ian Sellers, "John Howard Hinton, Theologian," *Baptist Quarterly* 33, no.3 (1989): 119–132; George Clement Boase, "Hinton, John Howard (1791–1873)," in *Dictionary of National Biography, 1885–1900*, ed. Sidney Lee (New York: Macmillan, 1891), 27:7–8. See also Albert Harrison Moore, "A Brief Biography of the Three Hintons" (MCT Thesis, Baptist Bible Institute, New Orleans, 1925), 10–21. This dissertation is archived in the library of New Orleans Baptist Theological Seminary (NOBTS). I am indebted to Marni Thurm, the Librarian of Union School of Theology, Wales, who was able to track it down and acquire an electronic scanned copy. I am indebted to Eric Benoy, Librarian at NOBTS, for scanning this work and

most significant concerns are these: will his son be both able, that is, useful, and godly?

Hinton stressed labouring in the development of ministerial abilities. Leaning on God for success, he urged his son to be diligent in learning and improving his mind. To learn well, Hinton argued, will enable his son to teach the flock of God well. He entreated him not to lose sight of evangelism and sermon preparation, though, and to use every opportunity through meditation to be creating sermons in his mind. For Hinton, diligence in cultivating ministerial abilities will serve much better than natural genius.

Hinton also emphasized the need for godliness. To labour in his study to make excellent sermons, though important, is not the end goal. He must be personally impacted by his study. Only after seeing the glory of God in Christ, his own unworthiness, and the stunning beauty of salvation will he find a message to preach that is as "a fire shut in his bones" and cause him to delight in preaching. Only from this place can he genuinely be in a position to minister to anyone. Hinton also urged his son to practice the discipline of regular mediation. Meditation causes one to be "warmed by the devotion of a heart breathing forth benevolent wishes for our fellow-sinners." Filling his heart full of the riches of Christ will cause him to overflow of warmth and devotion to those he is ministering to and will lead to usefulness. Other morsels of practical advice were sprinkled throughout the letter.

Like much of the pastoral theology of the eighteenth-century Particular Baptists, a pressing concern was for both pious and useful ministers.[3] We

providing access to it.

Hinton's second-born son was also named James (1792–1793) but died of measles at twelve months old. For more on James Hinton, Jr. (III), see Hinton, *Biographical Portraiture*, 51; Timothy C.F. Stunt, *From Awakening to Secession: Radical Evangelicals in Switzerland and Britain 1815–35* (Edinburgh: T&T Clark, 2000), 283–285, 379; Tim Grass, "'The Restoration of a Congregation of Baptists': Baptists and Irvingism in Oxfordshire," *Baptist Quarterly* 37, no.6 (1998): 283–297.

Hinton's youngest, Isaac Taylor Hinton (1799–1847) also entered the ministry, but he was born several years later and would not have been at Edinburgh at the same time. For more on Isaac Taylor Hinton see William B. Sprague, *Annals of the American pulpit; or, Commemorative notices of distinguished American clergymen of various denominations, from the early settlement of the country to the close of the year eighteen hundred and fifty-five* (New York: Robert Carter & Brothers, 1860), 11:804–812; Lloyd A. Harsch, "From Publishing to the Pulpit: The Life and Ministry of Isaac Taylor Hinton," *Baptist History and Heritage* 54, no. 3 (2019): 6–15. I am indebted to Michael A.G. Haykin for bringing this article to my attention. See also Moore, "A Brief Biography of the Three Hintons," 22–32.

[3] According to Andrew Fuller, "eminent spirituality in a minister is usually attended with eminent usefulness" (Andrew Fuller, "The Qualifications and Encouragement of a Faithful Minister Illustrated by the Character and Success of Barnabas," in *The Complete Works of Andrew Fuller: Memoirs, Sermons, Etc.*, ed. and revised Joseph Belcher [Harrisonburg, VA: Sprinkle Publications, 1988], 1:143). On the pastoral theology of the eighteenth-century Baptists see Nigel Wheeler, *The Pastoral Priorities of 18th Century Baptists: An Examination of Andrew Fuller's Ordination Sermons* (Peterborough, ON: H&E Academic, 2021). On the concept of usefulness in particular Baptist thought, see Christopher W. Crocker, "The Life and Legacy

would do well to glean from this wise counsel of James Hinton, who was a shining example of what it looks like to embody both "eminent piety, and ministerial ability."[4]

Text
I feel all things else respecting you to be absorbed in the great question, "Will my son be an able, godly minister?" The highest literary honours are vanity compared with this. ... Never for an hour lose sight of these two things—eminent piety, and ministerial ability. Learn well, and you will teach well. Make preaching your great delight. Lay in a good store. Glean in every field. Be forever making sermons in your imagination. Stir up the gift that is in you, and lean on an almighty helper for success. I had rather see you a preacher than an emperor: I am ready to say, O God, grant me this one thing before I die ... Set before yourself the highest models of excellence. Think what Spencer, Pearce, and Doddridge were at twenty-three—neither of them men of genius, but of great goodness and diligence.[5]

Above all things, do not suffer a day to pass without seeking the Spirit of God to witness with your spirit that you are born of him. Get your heart full of all that can interest your hearers when it is brought forth. I had rather, if it must be so, that you should sacrifice literature than piety.

Let me entreat you, my dear son, never to lose sight for a single day of the work of an evangelist. Give the Lord no rest, till you find the message you have

---

of John Ryland Jr. (1753–1825): A man of considerable usefulness—an historical biography" (PhD diss., University of Bristol, 2018), especially 2–10, 268–270. On piety and usefulness see Crocker, "The Life and Legacy of John Ryland Jr.," 284–286.

[4] Hinton had an incredibly fruitful life and ministry. For example, the Oxford meeting house was enlarged twice under his care (1798 and 1819). Hinton was a co-founder of the Baptist Union and ran one of the most respected grammar schools in Oxfordshire. He was president of the Sunday School Society that he helped found in 1815. He was heavily involved with the Baptist Missionary Society. He was urged to replace Samuel Stennett at Little Wild Street Church in London as well as being asked to take over John Fawcett's Baptist Theological Seminary in Hebden Bridge. Additionally, the College of Rhode Island offered him honorary a Doctorate of Divinity, which he declined. For more on Hinton's piety, see *The Diary of James Hinton (1761–1823)*, ed. Chance Faulkner (Peterborough, ON: H&E, 2020).

[5] Thomas Spencer (1791–1811) was an Independent minister at Newington, Liverpool. He was ordained in June 1811 but drowned two months later. According to James Montgomery, "young as he was, the character of Spencer at the age of twenty, was such as even aged Christians might not blush to own ... As a Christian, he was fervent, holy, and humble ... his piety was the ardor of an unquenchable flame" (as cited Thomas Raffles, *Memoirs of the Rev. Thomas Spencer, of Liverpool* [Boston: R.P. & C. Williams, and Samuel T. Armstrong, 1814], 243, 256). I am grateful to Timothy Whelan, who identified Spencer and graciously provided biographical sources. See Timothy Whelan's biographical index at https://sites.google.com/view/dissenting-studies-1650-1850/biograph/s/spencer-thomas. The other two figures are Samuel Pearce (1766–1799) and Philip Doddridge (1702–1751).

received from him as a fire shut up in the bones, which must have vent;[6] till you equally dread and long to preach—the first from a deep sense of your own unworthiness, the last from an ardent desire for the salvation of souls; till you feel as Isaiah did when he said, "I am a man of unclean lips, send by whom thou wilt send"—and a live coal from the altar purify and quicken your lips, so that you exclaim, "Here am I, send me."[7] Nothing will grieve me so much as to have you habitually rejoice in proportion to the fewness of sermons you shall have to make: of all work on earth, ours will be drudgery or delight in the extreme.

An irksomeness in commencing the study of sermons should be exchanged for a zest, a perpetual activity of meditation, securing every thought that may turn to good account. Every morning's lesson might suggest a text, warmed by the devotion of a heart breathing forth benevolent wishes for our fellow-sinners. To this point also some reading—and all hearing—of sermons should tend. Lay hold particularly on every mode of illustration. Enrich your imagination. Store your memory. Give force and variety to your diction; manly cheerfulness to your address; and a freedom, approaching by degrees to an entire deliverance from the memoriter system, to your manner.

In your habitual converse with men of wisdom and learning remember the fine adage, Keep within compass. Assert nothing of which you are not master. Be the modest inquirer, and gain something from everyone you meet with. Qualify yourself for conversation on all points of literature, history, philosophy, and theology, and habituate yourself in common conversation to a chaste diction, with nothing of the pedant.

It is easier to procure invitations for a young minister, than it is for him to gain such a character in the congregation inviting him, as will secure his stay and usefulness among them. We are apt to boast when we gird on the harness, as though we were putting it off.

The popularity of many young ministers is very short lived, because they do not go on to add to their stock of knowledge and talent, and then the people cease to respect the understanding of their teacher.

The spirit of his office leads a minister to be always making sermons, whether he wants them or not. The labour of choosing out acceptable words, words of truth well arranged, becoming a master in Israel, will tell more indirectly than it does directly; and your great danger is that of giving way to a reluctance to compose. I do not wish you to read your sermons, but it is impossible you can write too many. Much of your usefulness must depend on your not having to preach over again sermons now so well known. I hope you will have several, yea many, written, that you would not be ashamed to print; and a stock that will

---

[6] Jeremiah 20:9.

[7] Isaiah 6:5.

render unnecessary the starving work to your own soul, and the disreputable work to others, of serving up nothing but hashed meat.

Book reviews

Alison Conway and David Alvarez, eds., *Imagining Religious Toleration: A Literary History of an Idea, 1600–1830* (Toronto: University of Toronto Press, 2019), viii + 268 pages.

This book focuses on a topic that has become central to the history of the Baptist tradition. While it contains a rich variety of content, it delivers rather less than its subtitle suggests. The volume does not present a "history" in a way that would be familiar to many readers of this journal, in which an idea is shown to emerge, evolve, and variegate, as in classic works on religious toleration by W.K. Jordan and John Coffey. Instead, as a collection of essays by multiple authors spanning contexts across almost two and a half centuries, this volume offers a collection of soundings into the development of the modern doctrine of religious toleration, mainly with a focus on the development of that idea by literary authors. Although its content is rather occasional, the material in this book is of a very high order.

In her introduction, Alison Conway explains that the project came together as a response to political pressures to define the limits of free speech, especially as it relates to religious or anti-religious expression. Illustrating the ways in which literary scholars may work at a distance from their colleagues in history, Conway argues that criticism has yet to move beyond the secularisation thesis--and so, as a consequence, this book sets out an important new research agenda. It does so in multiple ways.

Paul Yachnin's chapter on Shakespeare's (1564–1616) Shylock (in *The Merchant of Venice*) and early modern ideas of conversion does an excellent job of defying the teleological assumptions that often mar histories of toleration, developing recent work on Shakespeare's Catholic connections, even as he recognises that "the play has grown over time in the direction of modern wisdom, which is a wisdom that both embraces freedom and tolerance and that also participates in the remarkably durable forms of racial and religious hatred" (p. 25). Sharon Achinstein's chapter on Aphra Behn (1640–1689) reminds us that the term "refugee" entered the English language as a consequence of the Huguenot diaspora, and that it was the restoration governments of Charles II that made chattel slavery the official policy of the realm, and excluded religious dissenters from the opportunities of full participation in the English state while allowing them to participate in the quite extraordinary experiment in religious toleration that was developed in the English Caribbean.

Andrew McKendry's chapter on Milton's (1608–1674) *Samson Agonistes* (1671) moves from the observation that dissenters were legally "disabled" to think carefully and provocatively about the theme of blindness in early modern theology. Corrinne Harol's chapter on Margaret Cavendish's (1623–1673) *The Blazing World* (1666) shows how this experience in science fiction played with the suggestion that racial or cultural variety would work best in a culture with only one religion. Almost by way of response, Humberto Garcia's chapter shows how Daniel Defoe (ca.1660–1731) cautioned those admirers of Locke (1632–1704) *et al*, who compared the supposed tolerance of the Pax Ottomanica to the intolerance of western European states. Colin Jager reads Shelley's (1792–1822) *Prometheus Unbound* (1820) in terms of the secularising ideologies that emerged from the French Revolution.

The chapters of this volume that might be of greatest interest to readers of this journal include those by Elena Russo, David Alvarez, Joanna Picciotto, and Mark Canuel. Russo argues that the experience of French protestants could lead friends and colleagues in very different directions in their thinking about religious toleration: while Pierre Bayle (1647–1706) sustained his early commitment to toleration, for example, Pierre Jurieu (1637–1713) argued for the conversion of France by force. Alvarez focuses his work on Samuel Butler's (1613–1680) *Hudibras* (1663), a satirical account of English dissent that actually works to undercut the hierarchies by which religious intolerance is sustained. Among the least "literary" of the volume's contributions, Canuel thinks about Joseph Priestley's (1733–1804) arguments in favour of toleration, and his resistance to the aspersions of Edmund Burke (1729–1797). And Picciotto reconstructs early Methodist literacy and shows that Methodist "experiments in holy living were also experiments in toleration," precisely because of the reading material that John Wesley (1703–1791) and others promoted––for, as Wesley put it, "If you need no book but the Bible, you are got above St Paul. He wanted others too."

With a range of theoretical reference that stretches from Michel Foucault (1926–1984) to Jürgen Habermas (1929–) and Carl Schmitt (1885–1985), this book offers a series of well-informed and carefully argued interventions that should, as its editors hope, set a new research agenda in literary studies.

However, from the perspective of this lapsed literary critic, the project perhaps claims too much for the exceptional qualities of creative expression. It is not clear to me, as one contributor claims, that literature has an "uncanny ability ... to put its finger on the pulse of history" (p. 5). Similarly, other contributors may claim too much for the contribution to the common good that literary critics make. I'm not sure that "the practice of formalist literary criticism of religious satire" (p. 149) will really make much of an impact upon modern debates about the faith and freedom of expression, as another contributor hopes it might. But these chapters should certainly shape the way that other literary critics think about this subject--and there is much in this volume from which historians of religion can learn.

Crawford Gribben
Queen's University Belfast
Belfast, N. Ireland

Stephen Copson and Peter J. Morden, ed., *Challenge and Change: English Baptist Life in the Eighteenth Century* (Didcot, Oxfordshire: the Baptist Historical Society, 2017), xvi + 304 pages.

As I approached *Challenge and Change*, I anticipated a dry recital of English Baptist theology, numerical account of churches and memberships, and the other standard fare of such histories. Scanning the contents raised my hopes quite a bit. Ian Randall promises accessibility and scholarship in his foreword, which raised them even more. I found myself wishing I had read Raymond Brown's 1989 volume to see how this new anthology compares with it.[1]

Although they are not designated as such, *Challenge and Change* has two major divisions. The first three chapters cover the major Baptist groups of the eighteenth century: the Particular and General Baptists, subdividing the latter group into two separate chapters on the original General Baptists and the "New Connexion" Baptists led by Dan Taylor.[2] The remainder of the book deals with sociopolitical issues affecting all three groups including home life, education, interaction with other Christians, and engagement with the community and nation at large. The intended result is a broad overview of Baptist life in one

---

[1] Raymond Brown, *The English Baptists of the Eighteenth Century* (London: English Baptist Historical Society, 1986).

[2] It is interesting to note that Taylor himself preferred the spelling "connection" to the uniquely British "connexional," though chapter author J.H.Y Briggs gives no reason why (p. 63).

"long" century measured from William and Mary's "Glorious Revolution" in 1688 to Napoleon's defeat at the Battle of Waterloo in 1815.

Co-editor Peter Morden opens the book with a discussion of the Particular (Calvinistic) Baptists. He begins by observing that had John Bunyan not died the year before, he would have been glad to see the passage of the Act of Toleration in 1689 which allowed open Dissenting worship, though with significant restrictions still in place (p.2). At the start of the long century, Particular Baptists were on the decline, noted here and elsewhere in the book. This decline is attributed to "High Calvinism," or the minister's refusal to call to personal faith in Jesus Christ out of concern that hearers might make a false profession. High Calvinists such as Gill and others insisted that the Holy Spirit alone could convert the elect. It was, however, not High Calvinism alone, but lack of full civil rights in worship, frequent disruption of services, difficulty administering believer's baptism and others that caused the decline (p.7). About midway through the long century a Particular Baptist upswing began that was fueled by evangelical revival on both sides of the Atlantic. John Edwards fueled the English Particular Baptist revival as his ideas caught on with Andrew Fuller, William Carey, and others. Fuller's *The Gospel Worthy of All Acceptation*, inspired by Edwards, was a landmark publication that either spurred on or alienated many Particular Baptists. Morden attributes the rejuvenation of the Particular Baptists to the evangelical revival, saying that it inspired the formation of the Bristol Academy to educate ministers and associations, such the Baptist Missionary Society that sent Carey to India, and the Baptist Union of 1812.

Helpful to a better understanding of the Arminian Baptists (General and New Connexion) is the separate treatment of these groups (chs. 2 and 3). Standard Baptist histories covering a longer time frame generally lack the depth found in the second and third chapters of *Challenge and Change*. Emerging in 1770, the New Connexion General Baptists emerged as the General Baptists trended towards Unitarianism. J.H.Y. Briggs points out other differences, such as the use of hymns in worship, that distinguished New Connexion and General churches, yet they still had much in common such as underlying Arminian theology.

As indicated above, having identified the three major groups of Baptists, the remainder of the book discusses sociopolitical life of English Baptists. Christopher Ellis points out the Baptist participation in the wider vision of church life within Dissent that was formed "through free association in order to gather for the celebration of faithful worship and the encouragement of holy living" (p. 77). Ellis uses this commonality to relate very different liturgical practices among the groups, pointing out that Particular Baptist worship was like that of the Independents, except baptism. What was sung or if any singing was done at all differed widely. Discipline was practiced in all groups. General Baptists may not have sung, but New Connexion churches as well as at least some Particular Baptists did, especially in churches influenced by the evangelical revival.

The book's discussion of home life is challenged by the lack of available source material, especially the poorer members of Baptist churches for whom there are no records. The authors seem to have left few stones unturned in their searches for such material. The book provides useful insights into the areas of home life, interactions with the wider community, and education. Not surprisingly in a time of high infant and maternal mortality, families often had many children with few surviving to adulthood. For all, family life included worship at home and education for children if the family could afford it. Michael A.G. Haykin discusses theological education at length, from the impact of the Bristol Academy to the development of theological education in London. Discrimination against Baptists seems to have had as much to do with their growing success in trade and business as it did theological differences. This success comes as a surprise considering accounts in this book and elsewhere of the high rate of poverty among Baptists.

The remaining chapters on political involvement, culture, and engagement with other Christians provide helpful glimpses to help round out the reader's understanding of English Baptist life in the long century. James Bradley focuses on four main points of Baptist contact with national politics: parliamentary reform, the American Revolution, ending the slave trade, and the French Revolution. Not all Baptists were in lockstep on these issues, but the general flow involved the common thread of holding government accountable. Baptists generally supported the American Revolution, particularly because of the issue of taxation without representation. Parliamentary reform involved limiting the powers of Parliament and increasing representation by underrepresented (Dissenting) groups. Baptists joined the Quakers in pressing to end the slave trade on biblical grounds and supported the French Revolution until it turned violent.

One of the chief problems with *Challenge and Change* is its relative obscurity. Just four years in print, the book is nearly impossible to find from customary American sources and is currently available only from the Baptist Historical Society, its publisher. Once found, it is a veritable gold mine of information that fills in the gaps of more comprehensive Baptist Church histories.[3] Particularly helpful is Briggs' chapter on New Connexion General Baptists, both in understanding the group's origins and the more complex divisions between them and their Arminian brethren (see above). Also notable are the interactions between Taylor and New Connexion General Baptists in America, often ignored elsewhere. Briggs's account seems much more likely given the amount

---

[3] See for example, Tom Nettles, *The Baptists: Key People Involved in Forming a Baptist Identity*, vol 1: *Beginnings in Britain* (Fearn, Scotland: Christian Focus, 2005).

of interaction between Britain and North America.

Many histories, it seems, taking a longer view of English Baptist history, tend to gloss over the eighteenth century. Surely, one encounters such men as Gill, Fuller, and Carey and others, but this history contains hundreds of names of men and women who were intricately involved in and promoted Baptist (Calvinistic or Arminian) theology and values in that time. There is something to be gained just by finding a person of interest in the index and being able to determine more about the active period of life and involvement in Baptist ministry.

Another striking thread that runs through all the chapters is the degree of commonality between General and Particular Baptists. Family life, political interaction, education, response to and engagement with community have much in common. The primary distinction early in the "long century" whether there is a free offer of the gospel. Particular Baptists in the first half and many in the second half of the century were "High Calvinists" who strongly believed that men should not interfere with the Spirit's work of conversion. General Baptists, on the other hand, were by nature evangelistic, believing that God enabled people to choose salvation.

The impact of evangelical revival in both groups cannot be overlooked and highlights the degree of interaction between Britain and her North American colonies. The impact of Edwards on British Particular Baptist theology, especially in the theology and life of Andrew Fuller is almost surprising until one remembers that theological works were accessible on both sides of the Atlantic. It would seem from Morden's account in the first chapter that Fuller was a stack of evangelistic kindling just waiting for the spark from Edwards. The New Connexion group responded to John and Charles Wesley.

One rather strange note about Morden's discussion of the high Calvinist response to Fuller is the complete absence of anything to do with William Gadsby, whose name is all but missing from the book's index.[4] Source and secondary material on Gadsby is readily available and his interaction even in brief would have been an interesting addition to Morden's discussion, along with a mention that even a high Calvinist such as Gadsby included in his hymnal some of the hymns of Isaac Watts. The omission is forgivable considering space and the larger issues under discussion.

The glimpses of Baptist life and interaction with country and countrymen through whatever source material adds much to the discussion of the period. Additional surprises awaited in Haykin's discussion of education, such as the fact that until the Bristol Academy appeared on the scene in the latter half of

---

[4] Gadsby is mentioned by last name only in connection with his collection of hymns by Faith and Brian Bowers on page 246. David Thompson mentions him only briefly on page 278 in his association with Strict Baptist churches and the *Gospel Standard* magazine.

the century, Particular Baptists were largely without formal education. Through a separate study of Gadsby, I was aware that he had no formal education but did not realize that this lack also extended to many of his contemporaries. It is worth noting the scriptural prowess with which some these men preached. Even so, concern about the lack of education was a matter of growing concern and action was ultimately taken to the benefit of later Particular Baptists. Awareness of this need does not seem to have found itself equally in the General Baptist camp, which apparently relied on the Holy Spirit to take hold of the man preaching and saw education and sermon preparation as interfering in the Spirit's work. This look into education was a highlight of the book's second part and calls to mind the differences that exist among Baptists of today.

A question often comes to mind when reading about the social, cultural, and political lives of a group of people within a given society and time: how do they compare to their contemporaries? For example, Karen Smith's chapter "Baptists at Home" discusses the challenges of high mortality rates and lack of good medical care available to Baptist families. One wonders that but for general wealth or poverty, how the lack of good care affected Anglicans, Presbyterians, Quakers, and others such as atheists at the same time. In other words, what makes these issues uniquely Baptist? If they are, it would help to clarify the distinctives. It is far easier to tease out the differences in educational structures and the matters of great political concern to Baptists over against others than it is to differentiate among activities of daily living. Smith calls attention to the general lack of source material, a challenge that surely faced Faith and Brian Bowers in their discussion of Baptist laity since the chapters overlap significantly. Timothy Wheelan makes a stronger case for distinction between Baptists and others in his chapter on culture. He is answering the accusation that Baptists made few cultural contributions, and thus his reviews of Baptist contributions to art, music, literature, and other areas. Some of his response strikes as spreading too little butter over too much bread where, for example, he speaks of Baptist Painters (p. 217). Overall, the discussion helps even a modern Baptist get over the idea that English Baptists were stiff and stodgy.

These overlapping discussions call forth another observation about the book's structure. It is understandable in an edited collection of essays covering the same main subject and time that the different authors will repeat some ideas, especially when a paucity of material makes it necessary to range farther from the main topic. I have already pointed out the overlap between Smith and the Bowerses. Additional examples abound. Brief overlaps are useful, however in that they allow the authors to confirm each other's views. There are no readily identifiable disagreements. which would have been difficult to resolve.

An extensive search for other reviews of this book turned up only two: one by Sheila Klopfer who welcomes the replacement of Raymond Brown's older work, and a second by Nigel Wright.[5] Aside from mentioning the lack of a bibliography, Klopfer has nothing negative to say. Wright, though familiar with the history, finds surprises such as the not-so-complete General Baptist slide into Unitarianism, along with some Particular Baptists who joined them. He also notes the cultural contributions over against Matthew Arnold's assertions to the contrary. In general, I agree with both assessments. The book is well-structured and contains vast amounts of useful information. It is engaging and friendly. Since the scope of the book does not include general English history to aid the unfamiliar reader, mentions of the Glorious Revolution, the Act of Toleration, and other things the editors assume the reader to recognize may prove challenging.

Individual chapters and the book overall are well-written, carefully-considered, and judging, as Klopfer does, by the footnotes, thoroughly researched. The examples given indicate a great familiarity with available source material and significant effort to find more. The best commendation I can give is that this book provides much deeper insight into the theology and lives of English Baptists than its 279 pages might make possible. It is a credit to each of the authors and the editors to have assembled this material into such a fascinating look into a time so very different from our own.

Brian K. Hart
Baptist Institute of Pittsburgh
Pittsburgh, PA

Roy M. Paul, *Jonathan Edwards and The Stockbridge Indians: His Mission and Sermons*. (Peterborough, ON: H&E Publishing, 2020), 193 pages.

Roy M. Paul not only introduces readers to the brief tenure of Jonathan Edwards in Stockbridge, Massachusetts, as a missionary, but he also provides insight into his pastoral care in a mixed racial parish. The English designed this community to ground the migratory Mohicans so that meaningful evangelism might occur. Paul shows how the spiritually-aware Mohicans came to see Edwards as a friend in spite of the tendency by other Englishmen to take advantage of the native peoples. In tracing the spiritual legacy of Edwards among the Mohicans, Paul begins with a history of the tribe, their spirituality, and their

---

[5] Sheila D. Klopfer, "Book Reviews: *Challenge and Change: English Baptist Life in the Eighteenth Century*. Edited by Peter Morden and Stephen Copson," *Baptist History and Heritage* 53, no. 2 (2018): 82–83; and Nigel Wright, "Book Reviews: *Challenge and Change: English Baptist Life in the Eighteenth Century*, edited by Stephen Copson and Peter J. Morden," *The Baptist Quarterly* 48, no.3 (2017): 142–143.

prized possession—the Stockbridge Bible. Jonathan Edwards' life and spirituality are then introduced to detail how he did ministry with the native Americans.

The first chapter gives a brief history of the Mohican tribe allowing their own historians to describe their origins. Drawing upon the resources of both primary and secondary material, Paul gives helpful commentary on the conflicting goals that caused the Indians to be suspicious of a joint venture with the English at Stockbridge. Avarice made for dishonorable trade agreements with the Dutch along the Hudson River. Nevertheless, the partnership was formed, a school established, and a minister called. This chapter helpfully chronicles the migration of the Mohican tribe from Massachusetts to Wisconsin, where they reside today.

Having spent time with the Mohican tribe in Wisconsin, Paul is able to speak to the current spirituality of which Jonathan Edwards was a spiritual father. The second chapter compares their historic belief in a "Great, Good Spirit" (p. 41–44) with biblical revelation and piety. While a comparative study, the purpose of this chapter is to highlight how the tribe transitioned to Christianity through the ministry of John Sergeant.

The Stockbridge Bible, a treasure of the Mohicans, has a remarkable provenience and story of its own, which needs to be told. Through the third chapter Paul discloses John Sergeant's appeal to England and the Prince of Wales's personal participation in the gift. The Bible's movement to and from Stockbridge is also described. The Bible now resides in Bowler, Wisconsin, at the Arvid E. Miller Library.

Building on the previous chapters as context, Edwards's abbreviated ministry biography is the focus of the next chapter. Through this chapter a case is made that Edwards was a good missionary-pastor in Stockbridge. First, Edwards seems to have been instrumental in the reduction of land grabs, even identifying himself with the Mohican by residing right in the middle of the village (p. 92–94). In buying small plots of land from the Indians, he was careful about how his dealings would look, but more importantly seemed to be communicating commitment to permanently reside with them. Edwards also became an informant to the Boston Commission of the corruption occurring in the school out of a concern for social justice. With the physical concern established, Edwards could demonstrate his distress for their spiritual well-being, which later chapters will develop. The balance of the chapter speaks to his spiritual sensitivity through his most famous sermon *Sinners in the Hands of an Angry God*.

The preceding focus on *Sinners in the Hands* serves to illustrate how Edwards did not drastically change his theological positions for a new audience. Instead, he changed his rhetoric and style to his new congregation. Sermons like *Things that Belong to True Religion* illustrate a continuity of spiritual concern, and subsequent sermon examples provide a reasonable suggestion of adaptation to his audience through the use of narrative and metaphor.

Overall, this is a valuable resource that brings together various streams of Edwardsean *foci* and will no doubt stimulate more areas for research. Paul also approaches the sensitive topic of social justice, demonstrating that Edwards was a complicated person. While the book does not address the problem of Edwards owning slaves, the book increases the tension to show Edwards in action to alleviate the suffering of the Indians. Paul's work will prove beneficial to expand the conversation on the existential changes occurring in Edwards as he interacted cross-culturally on the Massachusetts' frontier.

John S. Banks
PhD candidate
Vrije Universiteit Amsterdam
Amsterdam, The Netherlands

Eric C. Smith, *Oliver Hart and the Rise of Baptist America* (New York: Oxford University Press, 2020), 337 pages.

For Baptists in America, the long eighteenth century proved to be nothing short of transformative in terms of sheer growth as well as denominational maturation. In *Oliver Hart and the Rise of Baptist America*, Eric C. Smith traces the story of Baptist development in America throughout this period by looking at one of the foremost exponents of the "Baptist interest," Oliver Hart (1723–1795).

As the longtime pastor of First Baptist Church of Charleston, Oliver Hart has long been regarded as one of the most influential leaders who steered Baptist development in the American South. According to Smith, Hart's contribution "extended far beyond the Baptist South" as he sought to unite all Baptists on the continent (p. 5). The Charleston pastor not only worked to overcome geographical challenges to Baptist unity, but he proved to be instrumental in bringing together Separate and Regular Baptists, creating a denominational infrastructure, gaining respectability, securing religious liberty, and encouraging revival.

Smith begins his saga of Hart's life and ministry by situating the Charleston preacher within his family context. His grandfather was a Quaker turned Baptist in colonial Pennsylvania. Thus, Hart was steeped in the tradition of the Pennepek Baptist Church and the Philadelphia Association from an early age.

However, as Smith details, Hart experienced conversion in 1740 not through the ordinary ministry of the colonial Particular Baptists, but through the extraordinary revivals associated with the Great Awakening. Within Hart a synthesis emerged between the traditional theology and practice of his Calvinistic Baptist forebearers and the evangelical emphasis on conversion and revival associated with the Awakening.

Having been affirmed in his fitness for ministry, the Pennsylvania native accepted a call to pastor a fledgling conversation in the south, Charleston Baptist Church. With few Baptist works in the South at the time, Hart "purposed to establish a strategic beachhead for Baptist life in the South, importing the model of moderate revivalism and Baptist denominal order he had experienced in the Philadelphia Association" (p. 80). Under his labor and leadership, the Charleston Baptist Church grew in both size and influence. As Smith demonstrates, Hart did not limit his efforts to the local church but initiated the "first denomination meeting among Baptist churches of the South" when he led in the formation of the Charleston Association in 1751 (p. 105). Having solidified his church and established an association, Hart's prayers for an awakening were answered in 1754 when revival broke out in Charleston. As seasons of revival swept through the colonies during the mid-eighteenth century, Hart became known for his leadership and support of the evangelical awakening.

As revival gave way to the American Revolution, Hart never wavered in his support for independence. Demonstrating his notoriety, the Charleston pastor was asked to engage in a tour through the backcountry of his state to convince Loyalists to support the cause of the Patriots. Due to his vocal support of the Revolutionary cause, Hart was forced to flee Charleston upon its capture in 1780. He returned to his native Philadelphia area, where he was asked to fill the pulpit of the Hopewell Baptist Church of New Jersey. Following the war, Hart made the difficult decision to remain at Hopewell where he continued to promote the Baptist cause. While he would never return to Charleston, Smith sums up hart's influence well when he writes: "the center of gravity for Baptist America was beginning to shift from North to South, due in no small part to Hart's own labors in Charleston" (p. 277–278).

Near the end of 1795, the aging Hart breathed his last. While he had accomplished much for Baptists within his lifetime, Smith demonstrates that Hart's vision for widespread Baptist cooperation would come to be fulfilled in the formation of the Triennial Convention, the Southern Baptist Convention, and The Southern Baptist Theological Seminary.

In *Oliver Hart and the Rise of Baptist America*, Smith has written both an engaging biography of an influential Baptist leader and a gripping narrative of a rise of a denomination within the eighteenth-century American religious landscape. Each chapter situates a portion of Hart's life within the surrounding context in order to introduce readers to the larger religious currents within which American Baptists found themselves. For example, in chapter two, which focuses on Hart's conversion, Smith weaves Hart's story within the larger context of the Great Awakening. Thus, readers are left not only with an engaging personal narrative but also with a helpful survey of the period in view.

Smith's well-researched and lucidly-written work fills a major lacuna in Baptist studies by providing a focused history of eighteenth-century American Baptist development. Furthermore, by focusing on the life and ministry of Oliver Hart and his promotion of the "Baptist interest," Smith tells a multi-faceted story that captures both the denominational history as well as the realities of everyday existence as lived by one leading exponent. *Oliver Hart and the Rise of Baptist America* deserves a wide reading among historians of the period as well as those who maintain some affinity with the denomination "covered in Hart's fingerprints" (p. 314).

Dustin Bruce
Boyce College
Louisville, KY

Obbie Tyler Todd, *The Moral Government Theory of Atonement: Re-Envisioning Penal Substitution* (Eugene, OR: Wipf and Stock, 2021), 224 pages.

Obbie Tyler Todd attempts to do what no one has dared to do before—to consolidate the atonement thinking of the New England School of Theology. There have been many surveys and genetic studies prior to Todd's recent work; however, none that simplifies the theory without distortion. Indeed, it is a difficult task because each subsequent Edwardsean was an independent thinker with different nuances on the atonement. Todd, who is a prolific writer, takes a valiant stab at this daunting task. His work is divided into three major sections: origins, principles, and critique.

The origins section introduces the reader to the natural connections between Jonathan Edwards and his students. Yet, for the promised connection to Edwards of this section in general, it is deficient in making a direct correspondence between Edwards and his successors *on the atonement*. Rather than engaging Edwards as a primary source, Todd engages with secondary sources to create a sense of Edwards' view on the atonement. Todd assumes that the heirs of Edwards had reworked their mentor's thoughts; and this may be true, but there is no real engagement with Edwards' thinking on the atonement directly to arrive at this conclusion. From an historical perspective, Todd does do a good job situating the atonement thinking in the American context but does not make a clear enough contrast with European thinking on the atonement. For Todd, the public theology of the era is the *reason d'être* for the new thinking on the atonement.

In the next major section, which is divided into four chapters, Todd enumerates five general principles that define the Edwardsean thinking on the atonement. This reviewer would have encouraged Todd to introduce these principles earlier in the volume and tied them to Edwards Sr. or show how they differed. In his chapter on glory and goodness as twin principles, Todd excels in the exposition of the public nature by which God's glory is seen in the atonement. However, the chapter seems to take a tangent when discussing God's goodness. Bringing John Piper, as a disciple of Edwards, into the conversation on God's goodness seems to be out of place for the very fact that Piper is not a contemporary of the era Todd is examining. Piper is contrasted with Hopkins, but Todd might have done better by contrasting Edwards Jr. with Hopkins on "disinterested benevolence." Edwards Jr. had at one time corresponded with Hopkins to advise him on this topic. The remaining principles are developed well by the fifth principle, and when the reader arrives at this point, he or she is likely to have a clearer picture of the innovative nature of this thinking about the atonement.

In the final section, a critique is provided by contrasting this American thinking about the atonement with that of traditional penal substitution. Since the penal substitutionary model will be more familiar to most readers, this section will prove to be rewarding. To engage with the atonement thinking of the Edwardseans, he enlists J.I. Packer's delineation of the nine elements of the penal substitutionary model. This is probably one of the most fruitful sections of this book. After this analysis, Todd advances Oliver Crisp's view that there is a kind of penal substitution in the moral governmental view. As the book concludes, Todd sets up several ways in which the governmental theory can address difficulties associated with the traditional penal approach. In a culture that looks at victimization and hatred as vices to be avoided, the moral governmental theory provides a way to preserve God's honor by refocusing the atonement along the lines of vindication and justice. Todd makes a strong case for a "robust" atonement theory, which is inclusive of elements of this New England theory. Overall, despite a few criticisms, it is a good introduction to the thinking of the New England theology on the atonement from the mid-eighteenth century through to the late nineteenth century.

John S. Banks
PhD candidate
Vrije Universiteit Amsterdam
Amsterdam, The Netherlands

Matthew E. Roe, compiled and ed., *Preaching Deliverance to the Captives: Particular Baptist Sermons on the Abolition of the Slave Trade* (N.p., 2021), 213 pages.

One of the most amazing developments in the long eighteenth century has to be the moral and philosophical struggle waged by British abolitionists against the slave trade and slavery. And critical to its success was the key rôle played by British evangelicals. The name of the Anglican evangelical abolitionist William Wilberforce (1759–1833) is justly famous in this regard. But there were a multitude of others who also made significant contributions to the struggle. This newly-published volume of sermons on the abolition of the slave trade by five Particular Baptist pastors is revelatory of one of these significant contributions, that of the Particular Baptists.

Matthew E. Roe, who has self-published these sermons, places them in context in a detailed introduction (pp. 3–23). He shows the way that these sermons represent not simply the views of five individual pastors, but those of an entire denomination. Roe begins with the citation of texts from three Baptist associations—the Northamptonshire, the Western, and the Yorkshire and Lancashire—that reveal what one of them called "our deepest abhorrence" of the slave trade (p. 5). The concurrence of individual Baptists such as Martha Gurney (1733–1816), William Carey (1761–1834), Robert Hall, Jr. (1764–1831), John Rippon (1751–1836), and John Collett Ryland (1723–1792) in this detestation are also detailed (p.6–13). Roe notes key themes in the sermons, such as the inherent equality of all human beings, the duty of Christians to promote benevolence, and the utter injustice of the African slave trade (p.13–17). Despite the common Particular Baptist concern about bringing politics into the pulpit, these preachers were convinced that they had to speak to this issue, for it was a moral issue, not a political one *per se* (p. 19–21).

The five sermons—preached by Robert Robinson (1735–1790), James Dore (1763–1825), John Beatson (1743–1798), Abraham Booth (1734–1806), and John Liddon (d.1825)—were all preached within a five-year span, from 1788 to 1792, a period of intense activity by the abolitionists to secure the end of the slave trade. It was to be another fifteen years, though, before Parliament abolished the "diabolical traffic" (the words of John Liddon, p. 190). They are all reproduced in full with a minimum of editing. Each of them is introduced by a biographical sketch of the preacher. Following each sermon Roe has assembled various critical reviews that appeared when these sermons were first published. A few of these reviews are quite critical. For my part, however, each of these sermons is a gem and together they provide a fabulous window onto the way scriptural reasoning was the primary influence shaping the arguments of these abolitionists. The sermons by Dore and Booth are especially powerful in their exegesis and application. That by Robinson is probably the weakest of the five. It was preached during the closing years of his life when he was theologically confused—"ruined by pride" was the estimation of the evangelical Anglican John Berridge (1716–1793) (p. 31).

Central to Roe's publishing of these sermons is a desire "to inspire the modern reader when approaching similar issues today." Slavery and trafficking in human persons still exist in the modern world, as well as "other forms of injustice" and "disturbing scenes of oppression." And these call for the exercise of Christian benevolence (p. 22). These eighteenth-century preachers do indeed give us a great model to follow. Moreover, though Roe does not mention this, they also provide a substantial critique of some Christians in our day, who wish to mount a defence of slavery. Simply put, their arguments would astonish these Baptist preachers, who are generally far better guides to Scripture and Christian practice.

Michael A.G. Haykin
The Southern Baptist Theological Seminary
Louisville, KY

Timothy Larsen, ed. *Every Leaf, Line, and Letter: Evangelicals and the Bible from the 1730s to the Present* (Downers Grove, IL: InterVarsity Press, 2021), 328 pages.

The Bebbington quadrilateral has been invaluable to the historical study of Evangelicalism. In this volume, editor Timothy Larsen has collected a variety of papers focusing in particular on one point from the quadrilateral: biblicism. Having its origins in a 2019 conference held at Baylor University in honour of David Bebbington, this volume contains a diverse collection of studies from a variety of scholars, all looking at the various ways in which the Bible has been viewed and used by different Evangelical communities from the 1730s to the present.

Following chronological guides, the book is divided into four parts, each dedicated to a different century. The book is helpfully framed by an introduction and acknowledgement by Thomas Kidd and closes with general and scriptural indexes. Several of the chapters deal with Evangelicalism in America, but there are also chapters on Britain and New Zealand, and the final chapter by Brian Stanley looks at the "Global Context." Some of the chapters, such as Larsen's "Liberal Evangelicals and the Bible," which documents the fall of liberal

Evangelicalism and the subsequent rise of conservative Evangelicalism led by John Stott, are encouraging. Others, however, such as Mark Noll's chapter "Missouri, Denmark Vesey, Biblical Proslavery, and a Crisis for *Sola Scriptura*," serve as a reminder of some of the horrors that have been supported by Evangelicals. And still others, like Mary Riso's "Josephine Butler's Mystic Vision and Her Love for the Jesus of the Gospels," help to show some of the diversity in the history of Evangelical spirituality and practice. Throughout the book, one may find some of the chapters to be more engaging than others, but the collection as a whole offers a large and diverse range of topics, and readers of all types will find something of interest.

One small issue with the editing of the book, however, concerns the consistency in formatting. It is unclear why chapters one and six conclude with a bibliography, while the other chapters do not. It is also notable that seven of the chapters are divided by sub-headings, while the other five are not. These discrepancies are minor to be sure, but for the sake of readability and consistency, it would have been nice if all the chapters included both bibliographies and sub-headings.

Despite this minor note, this work provides an excellent collection of essays on a core theme in Evangelicalism. It will be of interest to a wide range of readers, from the lay person to the academic, serving at times as an encouragement, and at others as a sober reminder of massive blind spots. *Every Leaf, Line, and Letter* presents contemporary Evangelicals with a look at the diversity of our history, and can offer a hope for the future, as long as we are willing to learn from our past.

Jonathan N. Cleland
PhD student, Knox College
University of Toronto
Toronto, ON

CENTER *for* BAPTIST STUDIES
at THE SOUTHERN BAPTIST THEOLOGICAL SEMINARY

The Andrew Fuller Center for Baptist Studies, located at The Southern Baptist Theological Seminary in Louisville, Kentucky, seeks to promote the study of Baptist history as well as theological reflection on the contemporary significance of that history. The center is named in honor of Andrew Fuller (1754–1815), the late eighteenth- and early nineteenth- century English Baptist pastor and theologian, who played a key role in opposing aberrant thought in his day as well as being instrumental in the founding and early years of the Baptist Missionary Society. Fuller was a close friend and theological mentor of William Carey, one of the pioneers of that society.

The Andrew Fuller Center holds an annual two-day conference in September that examines various aspects of Baptist history and thought. It also supports the publication of the critical edition of the Works of Andrew Fuller, and from time to time, other works in Baptist history. The Center seeks to play a role in the mentoring of junior scholars interested in studying Baptist history.

andrewfullercenter.org

DE GRUYTER

The Andrew Fuller Works Project
It is with deep gratitude to God that The Andrew Fuller Center for Baptist Studies announces that the publishing house of Walter de Gruyter, with head offices in Berlin and Boston, has committed itself to the publication of a modern critical edition of the entire corpus of Andrew Fuller's published and unpublished works. Walter de Gruyter has been synonymous with high-quality, landmark publications in both the humanities and sciences for more than 260 years. The preparation of a critical edition of Fuller's works, part of the work of the Andrew Fuller Center, was first envisioned in 2004. It is expected that this edition this edition will comprise seventeen volumes.

The importance of the project
The controlling objective of The Works of Andrew Fuller Project is to preserve and accurately transmit the text of Fuller's writings. The editors are committed to the finest scholarly standards for textual transcription, editing, and annotation. Transmitting these texts is a vital task since Fuller's writings, not only for their volume, extent, and scope, but for their enduring importance, are major documents in both the Baptist story and the larger history of British Dissent.

From a merely human perspective, if Fuller's theological works had not been written, William Carey would not have gone to India. Fuller's theology was the mainspring behind the formation and early development of the Baptist Missionary Society, the first foreign missionary society created by the Evangelical Revival of the last half of the eighteenth century and the missionary society under whose auspices Carey went to India. Very soon, other missionary societies were established, and a new era in missions had begun as the Christian faith was increasingly spread outside of the West, to the regions of Africa and Asia. Carey was most visible at the fountainhead of this movement. Fuller, though not so visible, was utterly vital to its genesis.

andrewfullercenter.org/the-andrew-fuller-works-project

H&E Publishing is a Canadian evangelical publishing company located out of Peterborough, Ontario. We exist to provide Christ-exalting, Gospel-centred, and Bible-saturated content aimed to show God to be as glorious and worthy as He truly is.

hesedandemet.com

www.ingramcontent.com/pod-product-compliance
Lightning Source LLC
Chambersburg PA
CBHW030913080526
44589CB00010B/289